Table of Contents

Prentice Hall

Realidades 2

Communication Workbook with Test Preparation

PEARSON

Boston, Massachusetts Chandler, Arizona Glenview, Illinois Upper Saddle River, New Jersey

Note: Every effort has been made to locate the copyright owner of material used in this textbook. Omissions brought to our attention will be corrected in subsequent editions.

Art Credits
Page 226: Ted Smykel; **Page 244:** Ted Smykel; **Page 253:** Ted Smykal; **Page 271:** John Burgoyne.

ISBN-13: 978-0-13-322577-8
ISBN-10: 0-13-322577-1
12 18

PEARSON

Prentice Hall Realidades 2

Writing, Audio & Video Activities

Boston, Massachusetts   Chandler, Arizona   Glenview, Illinois   Upper Saddle River, New Jersey

Table of Contents

Tema 4: Recuerdos del pasado

Tema 5: En las noticias

Tema 6: La televisión y el cine

Tema 7: Buen provecho

Tema 8: Cómo ser un buen turista

Tema 9: ¿Cómo será el futuro?

Nombre ______________________ Hora ________

Fecha ______________________

AUDIO

Actividad 1

As an icebreaker for the first week of school, a teacher asks his students to draw a poster that describes him or her. Listen as each student describes him- or herself and match each description to one of the bio-posters below. Write the corresponding number underneath the poster. You will hear each description twice.

______

______

______

______

______

Actividad 2

As a second-year Spanish student, David is helping in the school counselor's office during the first week of school. As Spanish-speaking students enroll, he asks their name and nationality. Listen to each conversation, then circle the native country of the Spanish-speaking student. You will hear each conversation twice.

1. Bolivia, Chile, Uruguay
2. Argentina, Paraguay, Uruguay
3. Honduras, Panamá, Nicaragua
4. México, Puerto Rico, España
5. El Salvador, República Dominicana, Venezuela

Actividad 3

After Alicia enrolls at the counselor's office, David offers to show her to her first class. As he walks her to class, he points out his friends to her and tells her what each is doing. Match the pictures with each description of his friends. You will hear each description twice.

A.

B.

C.

D.

E.

1. ______ 2. ______ 3. ______ 4. ______ 5. ______

Actividad 4

Look at the people pictured. Choose two adjectives from the box to describe each person or group of people and write them on the blanks provided. You may use each adjective more than once. Don't forget to change the adjective endings as necessary!

alto	**guapo**	**paciente**
atrevido	**impaciente**	**reservado**
bajo	**inteligente**	**serio**
deportista	**joven**	**sociable**
estudioso	**ordenado**	**trabajador**
gracioso		**viejo**

1. ______________ ______________
2. ______________ ______________
3. ______________ ______________
4. ______________ ______________
5. ______________ ______________
6. ______________ ______________

Actividad 5

Read the descriptions of the new students below and then write a complete sentence to describe each of them. Use at least three different adjectives in each sentence.

1. Marisol trabaja con niños que tienen mucha energía. Ella tiene 24 años y tiene muchos amigos.

   ____

   ____

2. Gabriel tiene 29 años y es profesor de italiano. Él estudia mucho y trabaja 12 horas al día. También corre mucho y le encanta montar en bicicleta.

   ____

   ____

3. Juanita y Nicolita son amigas. Ellas hablan por teléfono todas las noches. Las dos tienen el pelo bonito y largo, y estudiaron en universidades muy buenas de Boston.

   ____

   ____

4. A David y a Linda les gusta jugar al tenis todas las semanas. También trabajan mucho en la casa y en el jardín. Les gusta pintar y tocar el piano.

   ____

   ____

5. ¿Cómo eres tú?

   ____

   ____

   ____

Realidades 

Para empezar

Nombre ____________________ Hora __________

Fecha ____________________

WRITING

Actividad 6

Some students at school are talking about the things they and their families do on the weekends. Look at each sequence of pictures and tell what the subject does, using the present tense.

1. Ramiro ____
____

2. Mi familia y yo ____
____

3. Yo ____
____

4. Patricia y Chucho ____
____

Realidades 2 — Nombre ______ Hora ______

Capítulo 1A — Fecha ______ **VIDEO**

Antes de ver el video

Actividad 1

Imagine that you are a teacher and it is your first day of classes. Write four expressions you might use to address the class. The first one is done for you.

¡Buenos días!

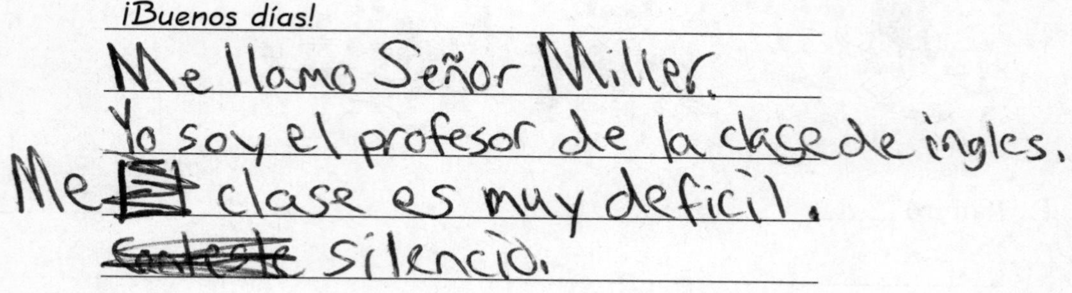

Me llamo Señor Miller.
Yo soy el profesor de la clase de ingles.
Me clase es muy deficil.
silenciò.

¿Comprendes?

Actividad 2

In the video, Esteban dreams he is a teacher. Circle the best choice to complete the sentences or answer the questions about his dream below.

1. En el video, Esteban es el profesor de
   - **a.** matemáticas.
   - **b.** español.
   - **c.** ciencias sociales.
   - **d.** historia.

2. ¿A qué hora empieza la clase de Esteban?
   - **a.** a las diez y cinco
   - **b.** a las nueve y seis
   - **c.** a las nueve y cinco
   - **d.** a las once y seis

3. En la clase de historia Esteban piensa dar un discurso sobre

a. los verbos regulares en el presente.

b. cómo hay que prestar atención al profesor.

c. los presidentes de los Estados Unidos.

d. la vida de George Washington.

4. Angélica y Lisa tienen que quedarse en la escuela después de las clases porque

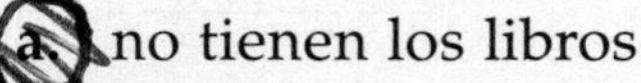

a. no tienen los libros.

b. llegan tarde a la clase.

c. hacen demasiadas preguntas.

d. no saben qué hora es.

5. ¿Cuál *no* es una regla de la clase de Esteban?

a. Los estudiantes tienen que estar en sus asientos cuando empieza la clase.

b. Hay que respetar a los demás.

c. Todos necesitan ir al armario.

d. Hay que prestar atención al profesor.

Actividad 3

Identify the speaker of each of the following quotes from the video.

1. Mamá, ¿por qué estás aquí en la clase? ____________
2. ¡Esteban! ¿Qué te pasa? ____________
3. Señoritas, ¿saben qué hora es? ____________
4. ¿Hay tarea esta noche? ____________
5. ¿Por qué estás delante de la clase? ____________
6. Lo siento. Pero se prohíbe ir al armario. ____________
7. ¿A qué hora llegas a casa después de las clases? ____________
8. Esteban, ¿qué es esto? ¿Tú eres profesor? ____________
9. Soy el profesor Ríos. ____________
10. ¿Qué pasa? ¿Dónde estoy ... ? ____________

Y, ¿qué más?

Actividad 4

All teachers have rules for their students. We already know Esteban's rules. Imagine that you are Esteban and write three more rules for your class.

____

____

____

Realidades 2 | Nombre | Hora

Capítulo 1A | Fecha

AUDIO

Actividad 5

Listen to these teachers welcoming their students to the first day of class. The pictures below correspond to things that the students must and cannot do in their classes. In the boxes under each teacher's name, write the letters of the pictures that correspond to what you must and cannot do in his or her class. There should only be one letter per box. You will hear each set of statements twice.

	Srta. Arcos	Sr. Cruz	Sra. Cazón	Sra. Rendón	Srta. García
No se permite					
Hay que					

Actividad 6

Listen as students talk about their classes this semester. Decide which class each one is describing and write the name of the class in the grid below. Then, place a check mark in the box below the class name if the student likes the class, and an X if the student doesn't like the class. You will hear each set of statements twice.

	1	2	3	4	5
Clase					
¿Le gusta (✓) o no le gusta (x)?					

Actividad 7

Teachers and students all talk about their classes with their friends and family. Listen to snippets of their conversations to see if you can determine whether it is a teacher or a student who is talking about his or her classes. Write an X in the appropriate box in the grid. You will hear each set of statements twice.

	1	2	3	4	5	6
Profesor(a)						
Estudiante						

Nombre _______________ Hora _______

Fecha _______________ **AUDIO**

Actividad 8

After listening to each of the following statements about school, decide whether it is **lógico** or **ilógico** and mark your answer on the grid. You will hear each statement twice. At the end of the exercise, you may want to compare your answers with those of a partner.

	1	2	3	4	5	6	7	8	9	10
Lógico										
Ilógico										

Actividad 9

Listen as a reporter for the teen magazine *¿Qué hay?* talks to students about their "secrets" for doing well in school. Fill in the grid below with their secret for each category: 1) **La cosa más importante para sacar buenas notas** (*the most important factor in getting good grades*); 2) **El mejor lugar para estudiar** (*the best place to study*); 3) **Si es mejor estudiar solo(a) o con amigos** (*whether it's better to study alone or with friends*). You will hear each set of statements twice.

	1	2	3	4
La cosa más importante para sacar buenas notas				
No tener televisor en el dormitorio				
Buena organización				
Dormir ocho horas				
Tener un profesor paciente que explica todo				
El mejor lugar para estudiar				
La cocina				
La biblioteca				
El dormitorio				
La sala				
¿Solo(a) o con amigos?				
Solo(a)				
Con amigos				

Realidades 2 Nombre Hora

Capítulo 1A Fecha **WRITING**

Actividad 10

Things are busy at school today. Look at the scene and write five complete sentences that describe what the people indicated are doing. One has been done for you.

Modelo *Manuel hace una pregunta.*

1. Sofía hace el proyecto

2. Roberto escuchar musica

3. Luisa entrega la tarea a la Sra. Sánchez

4. Manuel hace una pregunta.

5. Lidia y Vera juegan videojuegos a la computadora.

Realidades 2 **Nombre** ______________________ **Hora** ____________

Capítulo 1A **Fecha** ______________________ **WRITING**

Actividad 11

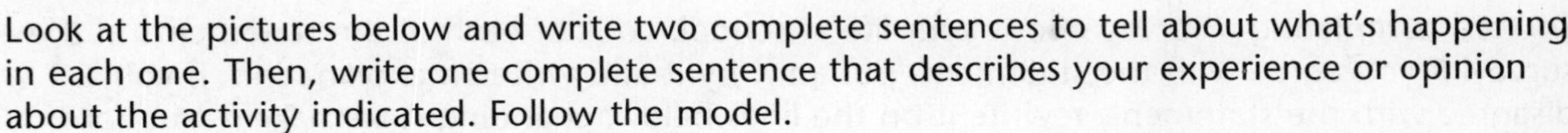

Look at the pictures below and write two complete sentences to tell about what's happening in each one. Then, write one complete sentence that describes your experience or opinion about the activity indicated. Follow the model.

Modelo

Los trabajadores de la cafetería sirven la comida .
Los estudiantes prefieren comer pizza .
Yo almuerzo a las once y media de la mañana .

1. ____ .
____ .
____ .

2. ____ .
____ .
____ .

3. ____ .
____ .
____ .

4. ____ .
____ .
____ .

5. ____ .
____ .
____ .

Actividad 12

You are completing a survey about your life at school. Look at each of the statements in the survey. If you agree with the statement, put an X by it and write an explanation. If you disagree with the statement, rewrite it on the lines below, changing it to make it true for you and your experiences at school. Follow the model.

Modelo X Hay muchas escuelas con más reglas que nuestra escuela.

Hay algunas escuelas que tienen menos reglas, pero nuestra escuela puede tener más.

_____ **1.** No conozco a nadie en mi escuela.

_____ **2.** Nunca tenemos tarea los fines de semana.

_____ **3.** Siempre prestamos atención en la clase.

_____ **4.** Todos los estudiantes sacan buenas notas.

_____ **5.** En la clase de español hacemos un proyecto cada semana.

_____ **6.** La comida de la cafetería siempre es buena.

Realidades 2 | Nombre ______________________ | Hora ______

Capítulo 1A | Fecha ______________________ | **WRITING**

Actividad 13

A. Look at the picture below of Universidad Troyana. Based on the picture, circle the activities in the bank that people do there.

leer	**estudiar**	**repetir**	**dormir**
bailar	**almorzar**	**pedir**	**poder**
jugar	**esquiar**	**servir**	**cocinar**

B. Now, using the verbs above, complete the ad below that some students are writing to attract people to the Universidad Troyana.

¡La Universidad Troyana es la mejor! Aquí, nosotros...

- ____.
- ____.
- ____.
- ____.

Para aprender más sobre nuestra universidad, lee lo que dice una de nuestras estudiantes:

"¡Hola! Yo soy Catalina, una estudiante de primer año aquí en la Universidad Troyana. Me encanta la vida aquí. Todos los días yo...

- ____.
- ____.
- ____.
- ____.

Realmente es la mejor universidad."

Antes de ver el video

Actividad 1

What extracurricular activities are there in your high school? When does each activity take place? Name at least five activities in your school and their schedules. Follow the model.

Actividades extracurriculares	El horario
club de español	*De las tres y media a las cuatro y media de la tarde, todos los lunes*

¿Comprendes?

Actividad 2

Put the following scenes in the order in which they occur in the video. Write **1** under the first scene and **7** under the last scene.

____

____

____

____

____

____

____

Nombre ______ Hora ______

Fecha ______

VIDEO

Actividad 3

Read the following descriptions of the students in the video. Then, write the name of the student being described in the space provided.

1. Es miembro del club de computadoras. ______
2. Trabaja después de las clases. ______
3. Le encanta el primer día de clases. ______
4. Es miembro del coro y de la orquesta. ______
5. Es deportista. ______
6. Es talentosa. ______
7. Tiene computadora portátil. ______
8. Según Lisa es misterioso. ______
9. Toma lecciones de artes marciales en un club atlético. ______
10. Quiere ser miembro del equipo de natación en el invierno. ______

Y, ¿qué más?

Actividad 4

Look again at the six extracurricular activities from **Actividad 1**. Survey your class to find out how many students participate in each activity. Then, record your findings in the table below. The first one is done for you.

Actividades extracurriculares	¿Cuántos estudiantes?
club de español	*Hay seis muchachos en el club de español.*

Actividad 5

As part of freshman orientation, students can go to the **Feria de clubes** to find the perfect club or activity for them. Write the number of the conversation next to the name of the corresponding club or activity that is being discussed by the two people. You will hear each conversation twice.

El club de ajedrez	______	El club de arte	______
El club de artes marciales	______	El coro	______
El club de baile	______	El club de fotografía	______
La orquesta	______	El club de computadoras	______

Actividad 6

What do Lorena and her friends do after school? Listen to the conversations they are having at lunch and place the number of each conversation in the grid under the corresponding picture. You will hear each conversation twice.

______ ______ ______ ______

______ ______ ______ ______

Actividad 7

Although they are best friends, Ana and Elisa are very competitive with each other. Listen as each girl tries to convince the other that her boyfriend (**novio**) is as wonderful as the other girl's boyfriend! Write the letter of the picture that corresponds to each part of the conversation. You will hear each part of the conversation twice.

A. 

B. 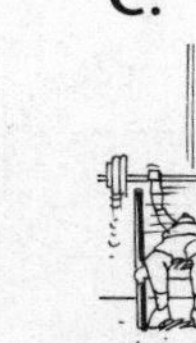

C. 

D. 

E.   

1. ________ 2. ________ 3. ________ 4. ________ 5. ________

Actividad 8

Javier's Mom does not know all of her son's friends by name, but she is familiar with what each one knows how to do well. Listen as she asks Javier about each of them. Match Javier's answers to the pictures below and write the name of his friend next to the picture. You will hear each conversation twice.

 ________________

 ________________

 ________________

 ________________

 ________________

Realidades 2 Nombre ______ Hora ______

Capítulo 1B Fecha ______ AUDIO

Actividad 9

We all know the expression "practice makes perfect." Listen as high school seniors are interviewed by a Hispanic radio station about the scholarships (**becas**) they received for their outstanding achievements in their extracurricular activities. Complete each sentence by writing the amount of time each of them has been involved with his or her particular interest. You will hear each interview twice.

1. Hace ______ que toma lecciones de piano.
2. Hace ______ que escribe para el periódico de la escuela.
3. Hace ______ que hace gimnasia.
4. Hace ______ que canta en el coro.
5. Hace ______ que participa en las artes marciales.
6. Hace ______ que crea páginas Web.
7. Hace ______ que toca el violín en la orquesta.

Realidades 

Capítulo 1B

Nombre ______ Hora ______

Fecha ______

WRITING

Actividad 10

It's time to submit biographies for the school yearbook. Answer the questions below based on the pictures, writing a complete sentence in response to each question.

1. ¿De qué club es miembro Rosa?

Rosa es un miembra de club

¿A qué ensayo necesita asistir esta tarde?

Necesito asistir para la banda

2. ¿A qué juegan Marcos y Jorge?

Marcos y Jorge juegan el ajedrez

¿En qué deporte participa Jorge también? ¿Y Marcos?

3. ¿Qué deporte le gusta a Mariela?

Mariela le gusta la natacion

¿Qué más le gusta hacer?

4. ¿Y tú? ¿En qué deportes o clubes participas?

Yo participo en futbol

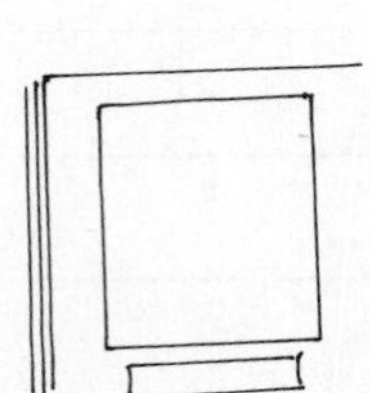

¿Qué te gusta hacer?

Me gusta leer

Nombre ______________________ Hora ______

Fecha ______________________

WRITING

Actividad 11

You are comparing all of the after-school clubs that you are thinking about joining. Look at their fliers below and write sentences comparing the clubs to each other. The first one has been done for you.

CLUB DE ESPAÑOL	CLUB DE FOTOGRAFÍA	CLUB DE AJEDREZ
Hay:	*Hay:*	*Hay:*
–27 miembros	–16 miembros	–16 miembros
–20 reuniones al año	–14 reuniones al año	–20 reuniones al año
–más de 8 actividades al año	–8 actividades cada año	–8 actividades cada año
Es:	*Es:*	*Es:*
–un club educativo	–un club recreativo	–un club recreativo
–un club para todos	–un club para todos	–sólo para personas inteligentes
Cuesta:	*Cuesta:*	*Cuesta:*
–12 dólares al año	–20 dólares al año	–12 dólares al año

1. *El club de ajedrez es tan popular como el club de fotografía.*
2. ______________________
3. ______________________
4. ______________________
5. ______________________
6. ______________________
7. ______________________

Realidades 2 | Nombre | Hora

Capítulo 1B | Fecha | **WRITING**

Actividad 12

Imagine that you are preparing questions for a Spanish-language game show. You are given topics and must produce two logical and gramatically correct questions about each topic: one using the present tense of the verb **saber** and one using the present tense of the verb **conocer.** Use the model to help you write your questions.

Modelo el alfabeto

¿*Sabes las letras del alfabeto en español*?

¿*Conoces el alfabeto español*?

1. Madrid

 ¿Sabes el presidente del Madrid?

 ¿Conoces a Madrid?

2. el ajedrez

 ¿Sabes jugar el ajedrez?

 ¿Conoces el club de ajedrez?

3. la natación

 ¿Sabes la regla de la natación?

 ¿Conoces el miembro la natación?

4. el libro *Don Quijote de la Mancha*

 ¿Sabes las personas del libro?

 ¿Conoces el libro Don Quitjote de la Mancha en espanol?

5. la música latina

 ¿Sabes cantar la música latina?

 ¿Conoces a música latina?

6. la fotografía

 ¿Sabes?

 ¿Conoces?

7. las reglas de tu escuela

 ¿Sabes?

 ¿Conoces?

Realidades 2 | Nombre ______ | Hora ______

Capítulo 1B | Fecha ______ | WRITING

Actividad 13

A. Imagine that you are preparing to interview the busiest student in your school, Alfonso, to find out how long he has been participating in all of his activities. Below is a list of things he does during the week. Write the six questions you are going to ask him. Follow the model.

soy miembro del club de ajedrez
hago gimnasia
ensayo con la orquesta
asisto a las reuniones del club de fotografía
participo en la natación
tomo lecciones de artes marciales
juego a los bolos

Modelo *¿Cuánto tiempo hace que juegas a los bolos?*

1. ¿______?
2. ¿______?
3. ¿______?
4. ¿______?
5. ¿______?
6. ¿______?

B. Now, write a paragraph about at least three activities you participate in and say how long you have been doing each of them. Supply at least two additional details about each activity. Follow the model.

Modelo *Hace tres años que juego a los bolos. Juego con mi papá los sábados y siempre gano.*

Realidades 2 Nombre ______ Hora ______

Capítulo 2A Fecha ______ **VIDEO**

Antes de ver el video

Actividad 1

What do you do every morning? In the table below, write at least five activities you do each day. One has been done for you.

Por la mañana...
Me despierto.

¿Comprendes?

Actividad 2

Decide whether each statement about the video is **cierto** or **falso.** If a statement is false, rewrite it to make it true.

1. Raúl y Tomás están muy interesados en el programa de televisión.

______

2. Gloria recibe una llamada de teléfono.

______

3. Raúl y Tomás quieren participar en una obra de teatro.

______

4. Hay una emergencia en el teatro y Gloria necesita la ayuda de tres personas mañana.

______

5. Tomás piensa que la experiencia puede ser interesante.

____

6. Tomás se ve mal.

____

7. Raúl tiene que lavarse la cara, cepillarse los dientes, ponerse desodorante y vestirse.

____

8. Los muchachos tienen cincuenta minutos para prepararse.

____

Actividad 3

Write the appropriate word or words in the spaces provided.

1. Raúl no se quiere poner tanto ____________.

2. Tomás pregunta: ¿Es necesario ____________ los labios?

3. La señora de maquillaje pide ____________ y ____________.

4. Esto fue idea de ____________.

5. Tomás le dice a Raúl que la ropa de payaso (*clown*) no es muy ____________.

6. Según Raúl la obra va a ser ____________.

Y, ¿qué más?

Actividad 4

Write four complete sentences to tell about your morning routine. Use the phrases in the bank. Follow the model.

me acuesto	**me ducho**
me afeito	**me lavo**
me baño	**me levanto**
me cepillo	

Modelo *Cada día, me levanto a las 7 de la mañana.*

____

____

____

____

Nombre ______________________ Hora ____________

Fecha ______________________ AUDIO

Actividad 5

Listen as a very frustrated mother tries to get her two teenage children, Luis and Catrina, out of the house on time to get to school. Each one gives her excuse after excuse. Look at the pictures below and match the number of the excuse you hear to each drawing. Write the number of the excuse on the line under the picture. You will hear each conversation twice.

Actividad 6

Listen to people talking about an upcoming event in their lives. Based on the conversations, decide what event each person is getting ready for. Place a check mark in one box in each person's row. You will hear each set of statements twice.

	Una cita para ir al cine	Un partido	Un concurso	Una audición	Una boda	Una fiesta
Chucho						
Gloria						
Gabriel						
Roberto						
Dana						
Marisol						

Realidades 2 | Nombre _______________ Hora _______

Capítulo 2A | Fecha _______________ **AUDIO**

Actividad 7

Listen as a young model and her photographer describe a typical weekend photo shoot to a magazine reporter. They will mention specific activities that they do at particular times during the day. Write the time of day that the reporter and the model say that they do each thing. Be careful! Not all of the squares will be filled for both people. You will hear this dialogue twice.

	La modelo	El fotógrafo
	6:00 A.M.	

Realidades 2 | Nombre ____________ | Hora ____________

Capítulo 2A | Fecha ____________ | **AUDIO**

Actividad 8

Parents are sometimes surprised to learn from teachers that their children act differently at school than they do at home. Listen to mothers, who are volunteering in the school today, as they talk to their children's teachers. How do the mothers view their children? According to the teachers, how are they acting today in class? Fill in the chart below with adjectives as you listen. You will hear each dialogue twice.

	Ana	Javier	Laura	Mateo	Linda	Joaquín
Según la madre, ¿cómo es su hijo(a)?						
Según el (la) profesor(a), ¿cómo está su hijo en clase?						

Actividad 9

Listen as Claudia's father tries to sort out all of the items left at their home after his daughter's friend Laura spent the night. As you listen to the conversation, sort out which items belong to Claudia and which belong to Laura. Under each picture, write the first initial of the person the item belongs to. You will hear this conversation twice.

______

______

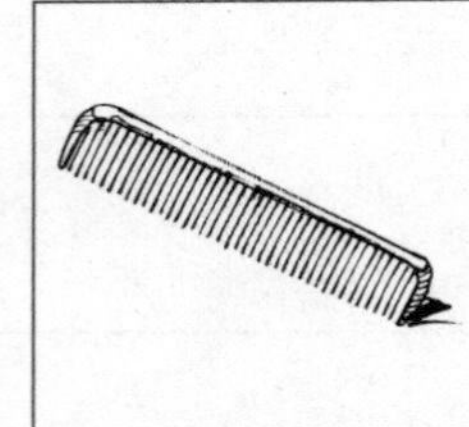
______

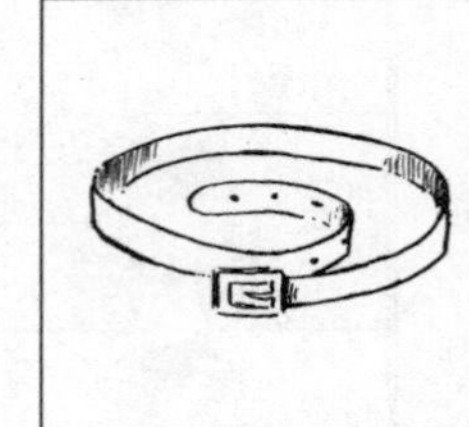
______

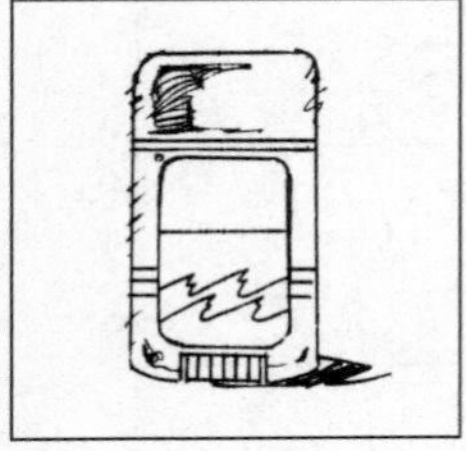
______

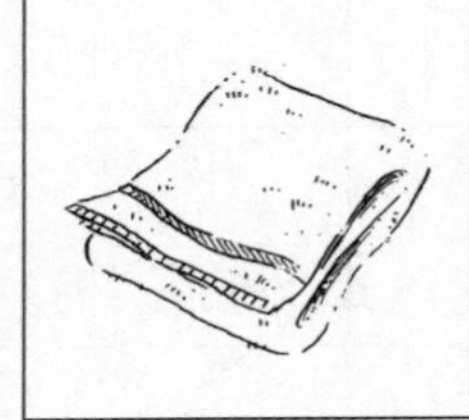
______

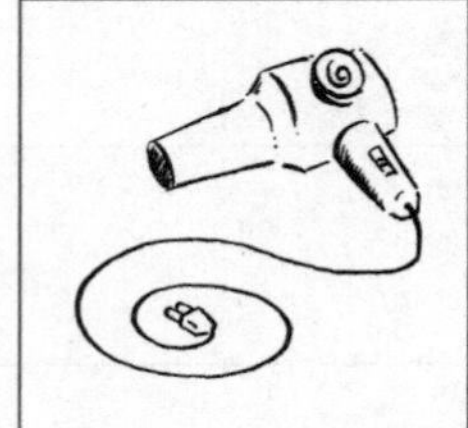
______

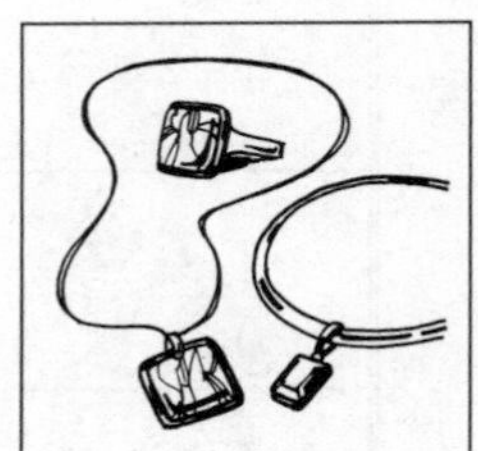
______

Actividad 10

Write complete sentences to tell what the following people have to do each morning and what items they use while doing these activities. Follow the model.

Pancho

Teresa and Lolis

Juanita

Alicia

Cristina

Raúl

Yo

Modelo *Pancho no tiene que arreglarse el pelo*

1. ______________________________
2. ______________________________
3. ______________________________
4. ______________________________
5. ______________________________
6. ______________________________

Nombre ______ Hora ______

Fecha ______

WRITING

Actividad 11

Esteban is never able to get to school on time. Describe what he does each morning, using the pictures to guide you. **¡OJO!** Some of the verbs are reflexive, while others are not. The first one has been done for you.

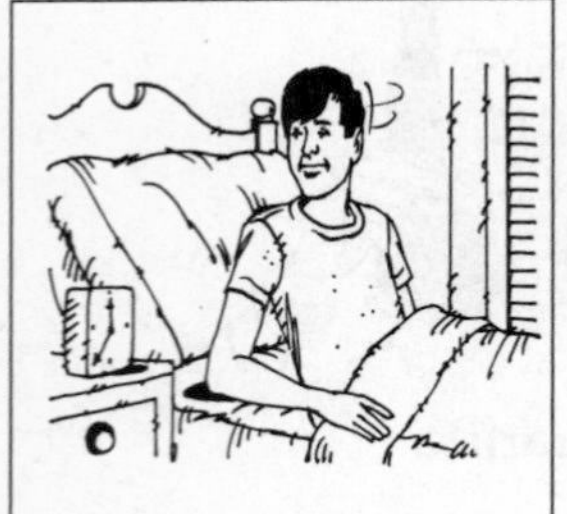

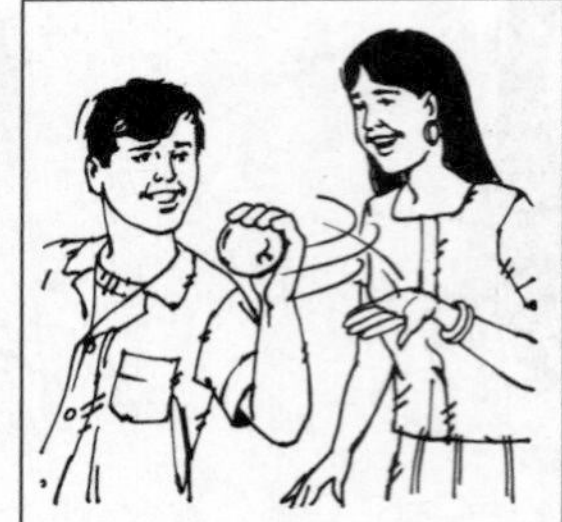

Primero, Esteban se levanta.

______

______

______

______

______

______

______

Actividad 12

The people below are on vacation. First, complete the questions about them and their trips by circling the correct verbs. Then, answer the questions in complete sentences.

1. ¿Dónde (es, está) Lola?

2. ¿De dónde (es, está)?

3. ¿Cómo (es, está) ella hoy? ¿Contenta?

4. ¿Cómo (es, está) ella? ¿Baja?

5. ¿Qué (es, está) haciendo en este momento?

6. ¿Dónde (son, están) los señores Obregón?

7. ¿De dónde (son, están)?

8. ¿Cómo (son, están)? ¿Perezosos?

9. ¿Cómo (son, están) hoy? ¿Tristes?

10. ¿Qué (son, están) haciendo en este momento?

Realidades 2 | Nombre ______ | Hora ______

Capítulo 2A | Fecha ______ | **WRITING**

Actividad 13

A. Think of the items you and your family members use every day. Which things are yours, which are theirs, and which are common to everyone in the family? Make a list of three items in each column.

Mine	My family members'	Ours

B. Now, write a descriptive paragraph about what you and your family members do with each of these items. Follow the model.

Modelo *Yo me arreglo el pelo todos los días con el gel mío.*

Realidades 2 | Nombre ______ | Hora ______

Capítulo 2B | Fecha ______ | VIDEO

Antes de ver el video

Actividad 1

Write seven sentences to tell about what kind of clothes you like to wear. Use the words in the box to help you.

la ganga	**la liquidación**	**el mercado**	**algodón**	**de cuero**
está hecho(a) de	**claro(a)**	**oscuro(a)**	**vivo(a)**	**apretado(a)**
flojo(a)	**mediano(a)**	**la talla**	**el dinero**	**el regalo**
el precio	**los pantalones**	**la blusa**	**la falda**	**la chaqueta**
tela sintética				

1. ______
2. ______
3. ______
4. ______
5. ______
6. ______
7. ______

¿Comprendes?

Actividad 2

Circle the correct response below.

1. 
Gloria ve un letrero que
   a. anuncia una liquidación fabulosa.
   b. informa al público de una tienda nueva.
   c. tiene el horario de la tienda favorita de Gloria.

2. 
A Raúl y a Tomás no les gusta
   a. ir al mercado.
   b. ir de compras.
   c. tomar refrescos.

3. 
Gloria compró una blusa que era
   a. de talla extra-grande.
   b. muy fea.
   c. una ganga.

4. 
Tomás quiere ir
   a. a casa.
   b. al centro comercial.
   c. al mercado.

5. 
Gloria exclama: "Aquellas blusas tienen
   a. un estilo muy bonito".
   b. unos colores aburridos".
   c. muchas tallas, pero ninguna me sirve".

6. 
A Gloria le gusta la blusa
   a. un poco floja.
   b. bien apretada.
   c. de cuero.

7. 
La blusa está hecha de
   a. lana.
   b. algodón.
   c. seda.

8. Gloria dice que
   a. Raúl es muy impaciente.
   b. Raúl es su hermano favorito.
   c. Raúl no se viste de moda.

9. Raúl
   a. tiene dinero para gastar, aunque le dijo a Gloria que no tenía nada.
   b. no tiene nada de dinero.
   c. le pide prestado dinero a Gloria.

10. 
Gloria paga por su blusa
   a. con cheque.
   b. en efectivo.
   c. con tarjeta de crédito.

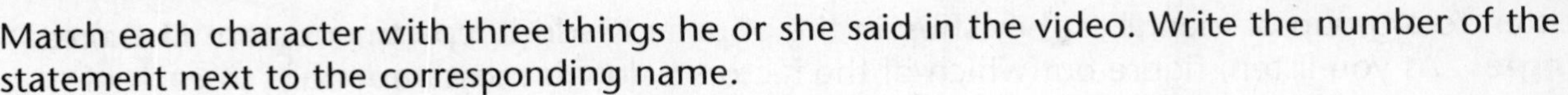

Realidades 2 Nombre ____________ Hora ____________

Capítulo 2B Fecha ____________ VIDEO

Actividad 3

Match each character with three things he or she said in the video. Write the number of the statement next to the corresponding name.

El personaje

Gloria _____ _____ _____

Tomás _____ _____ _____

Raúl _____ _____ _____

Lo que dice

1. ¡Una liquidación fabulosa! ¿Qué les parece?
2. Bueno, no me importa, pero creo que los precios son muy altos.
3. ¿Hay un mercado cerca de aquí?
4. ... por favor, ¿otra blusa?
5. Me queda un poco floja. Pero me gusta así...
6. ¿De qué está hecha?
7. ¿El precio? A ver... 9,400 colones.
8. Mira. Aquellas chaquetas de cuero.
9. Pero no tienes dinero.

Y, ¿qué más?

Actividad 4

Do you like to shop? Write a short paragraph telling why or why not.

Modelo *A mí no me gusta mucho ir de compras. A mi hermana, sin embargo, le encanta comprar de todo. Por eso no me gusta salir con ella. Pero cuando quiero comprar discos compactos, vamos al centro comercial. Yo voy a las tiendas de discos y ella va a las de ropa. Ella gasta todo su dinero y yo no gasto mucho. Lo mejor de todo es que al final puedo comprarme un helado.*

Nombre ______________________ Hora __________

Fecha ______________________

AUDIO

Actividad 5

Listen to a group of friends as they shop in the popular Madrid department store **El Corte Inglés.** As you listen, figure out which of the factors below is most important to each of them when deciding what to buy. Some may have more than one answer. Put an X in the appropriate column(s) for each girl. You will hear this conversation twice.

	El precio	La moda/ El estilo	La marca	La talla/cómo te queda(n)
Alicia				
Marta				
Carmen				
Luz				
Lorena				

Actividad 6

Some people enjoy shopping, while others find it frustrating. Listen to several conversations as people look for particular items in a department store. Match the conversations to the pictures by writing the number of the conversation it represents under each picture. You will hear each conversation twice.

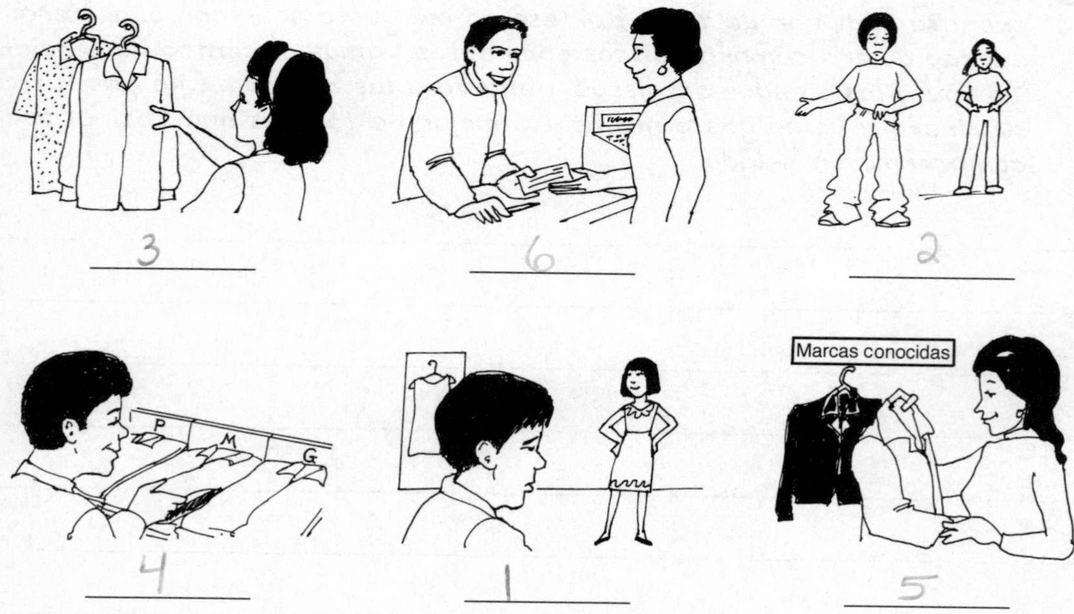

Actividad 7

Listen to the following teenagers describe to a radio announcer the most daring thing they have ever done. As the radio interviewer asks each one **"¿Cuál es la cosa más atrevida que hiciste?"**, look at the pictures below. Write the number of each response under the corresponding picture. You will hear each response twice.

______

______

______

______

______

______

Nombre ______________________ Hora ________

Fecha ______________________

AUDIO

Actividad 8

This semester, Eleanor is hosting an exchange student from Ecuador named Marta. Listen as they talk about different items in a department store. Based on each description, place an X on the line labeled A or B to indicate which one accurately represents what is said in each conversation. You will hear each conversation twice.

1.

A. ________

B. ________

2.

A. ________

B. ________

3.

A. ________

B. ________

4.

A. ________

B. ________

Actividad 9

Listen as Mariana shops for several gifts for her friends as well as a few things for herself. In each department she is able to narrow her choices down to two, and then finally makes her selection. In the spaces below, check off all the items that she decides to buy. You will hear each conversation twice.

1. 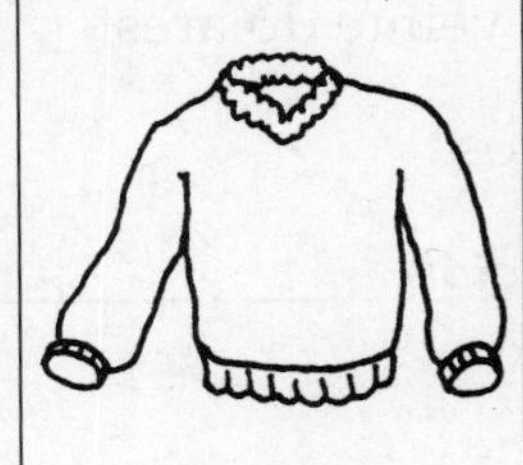 ____  ____

2. 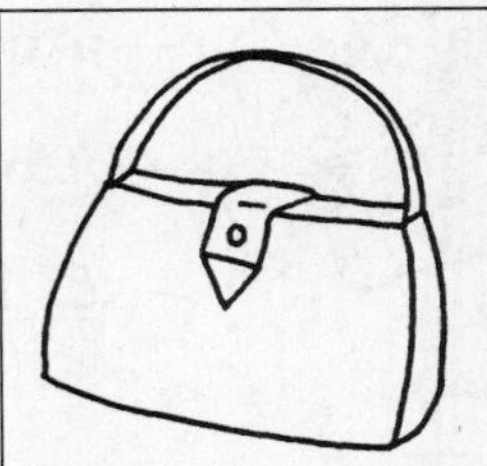 ____  ____

3. 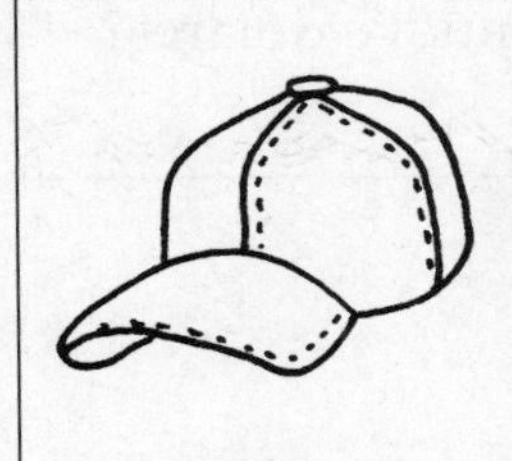 ____  ____

4.  ____ 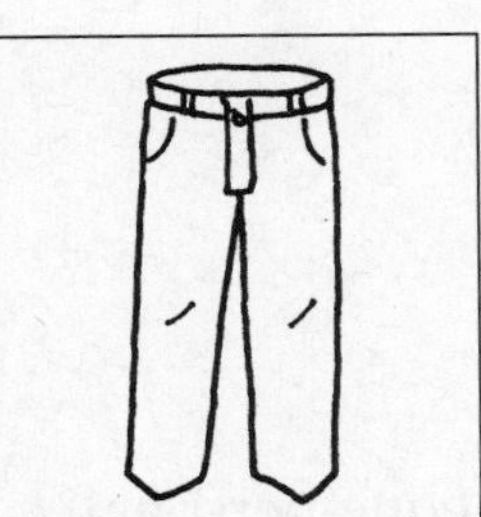 ____

5. 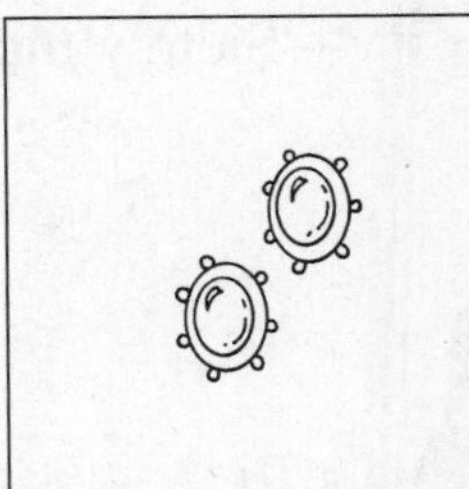 ____ 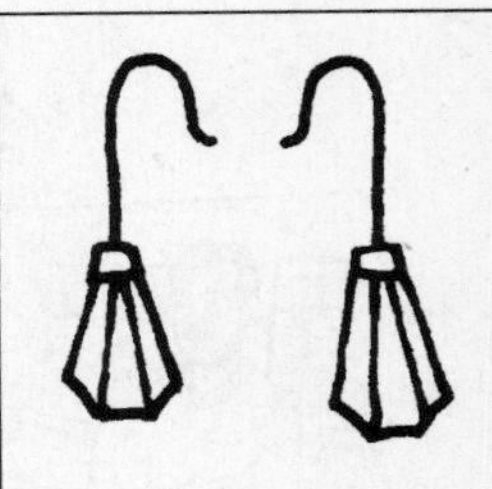 ____

Actividad 10

There is a sale at your local department store this weekend and you've run into many of your friends there, shopping for bargains. Complete the mini-conversations below.

Modelo

—¡Aquellos zapatos cuestan sólo veinte dólares!

—¿Cómo sabes que son tan baratos?

—*El letrero anuncia la liquidación*.

1.

—¿De qué color es el suéter que tienes en la mano?

— El suéter es negro.

—¿Y cuesta sólo nueve dólares?

—Sí, el suéter es nueve dólares.

2.

—Señor, me gustaría ver aquellos zapatos.

—Claro, señorita. ¿Cuesta dólares?

—Siete y medio.

3.

—¿Ud. paga con cheque personal?

—No, paga con la tarejta de credito.

4.

—Ramón, tengo unas camisas en colores pastel para ti.

—Gracias, papá, pero camisas vivos.

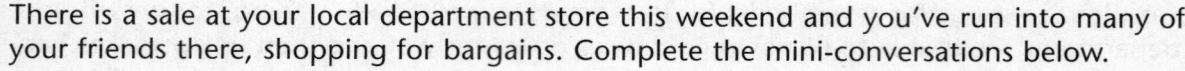

Realidades 2 | Nombre ______ | Hora ______

Capítulo 2B | Fecha ______ | WRITING

Actividad 11

Write complete sentences to tell what the following people did yesterday. Use the correct preterite form of the verbs suggested by the pictures. Follow the model and be creative.

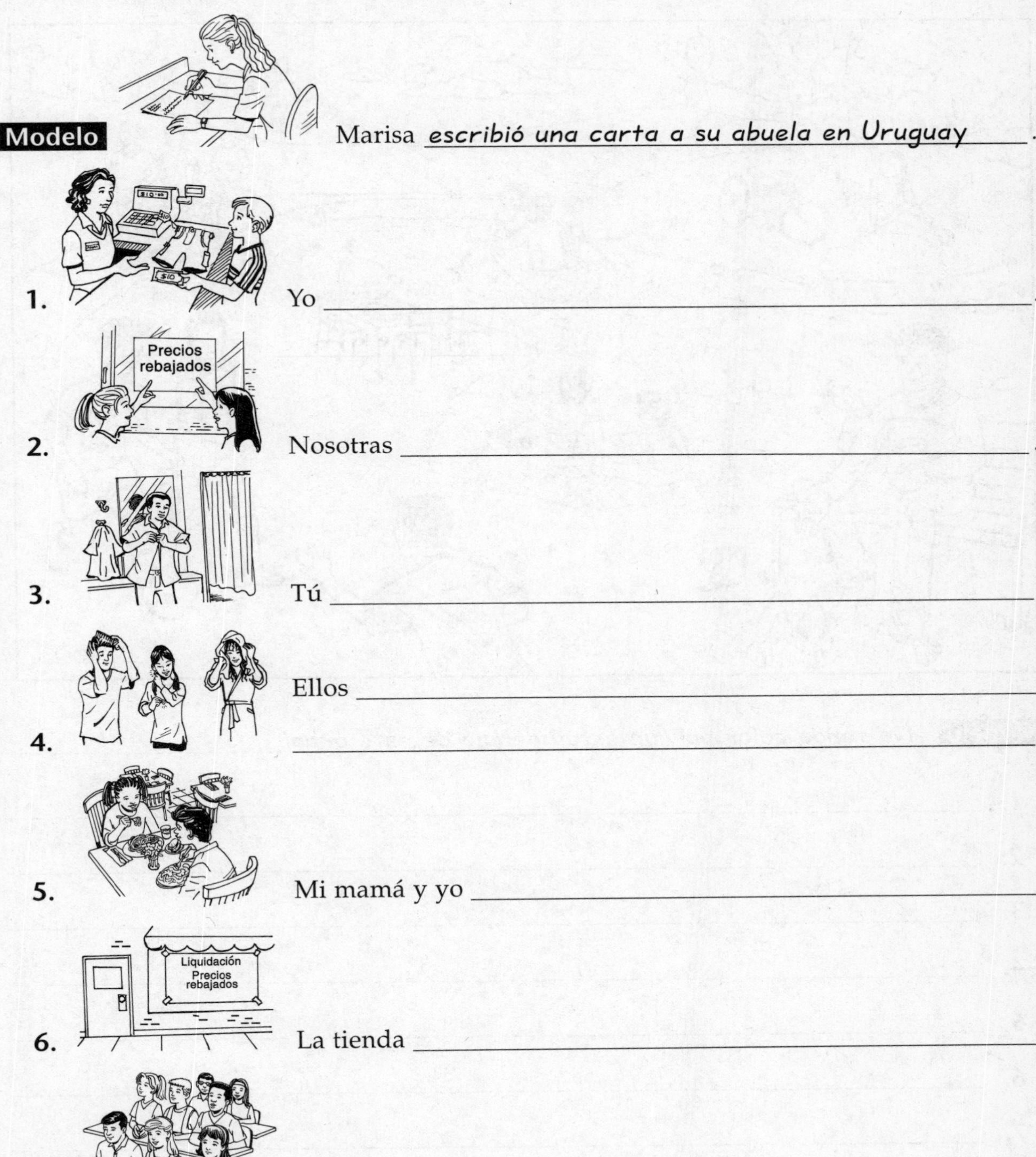

Modelo Marisa *escribió una carta a su abuela en Uruguay*.

1. Yo ______.

2. Nosotras ______.

3. Tú ______.

4. Ellos ______.

5. Mi mamá y yo ______.

6. La tienda ______.

7. Los estudiantes ______.

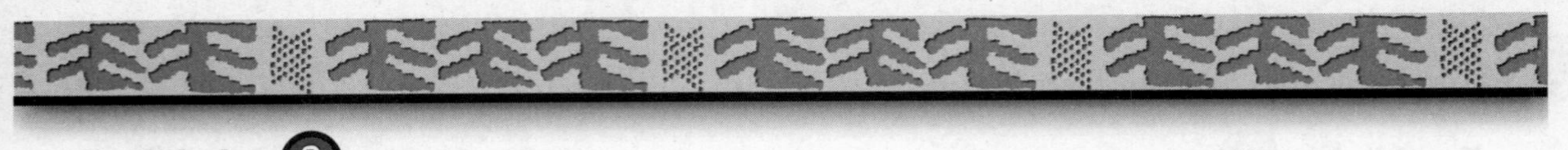

Actividad 12

Alicia is thinking about the things she sees around her in the park. Describe these items in relation to her in the picture using a form of **este, ese,** or **aquel.** Follow the model.

Modelo *No tengo calor porque estoy debajo de este árbol.*

1. ______________________________

2. ______________________________

3. ______________________________

4. ______________________________

5. ______________________________

6. ______________________________

7. ______________________________

Realidades 2 Nombre Hora

Capítulo 2B Fecha **WRITING**

Actividad 13

Imagine that the items of clothing below are yours. Describe each item and tell when you wore it last. Follow the model.

Modelo

Aquellos pantalones son diferentes. Llevé estos jeans cuando pinté la casa hace una semana. Llevé los grises a la escuela ayer.

1. 

2. 

3. 

Nombre ______ Hora ______

Fecha ______ **VIDEO**

Antes de ver el video

Actividad 1

Following is a list of things that the characters from the video did during the day. In the second column, write the place where they probably went to do each thing. The first one has been done for you.

Cosas que hacer	Lugar
ir a ver una película	*el cine*
1. comprar champú y pasta dental	el supermercado
2. llenar el tanque de gasolina	la estación de servicio
3. enviar una carta	el buzón
4. comprar unos patines	una tiende de deportes
5. comprar un regalo	el centro
6. comprar sellos	el correo

¿Comprendes?

Actividad 2

First, match each statement on the right with its corresponding picture, using the letters **a-e**. Then, number the scenes in each section in the order in which they occur in the video. Write **1** for the first scene and **5** for the last. One is done for you.

A. Teresa y Claudia

a. 

b. 

c. 

b Claudia habló con Ramón por el celular para ir al Bazar San Ángel. 5

______ Teresa escoge el champú que va a comprar. ______

______ Teresa fue al correo para comprar sellos. ______

Nombre ____________________ Hora ________

Fecha ____________________

VIDEO

d. ______ Teresa y Claudia se encontraron. ______

e. ______ Teresa necesita comprar varias cosas en la farmacia. ______

B. Ramón y Manolo

a. ______ El asistente llenó el tanque. ______

b. ______ Manolo y Ramón fueron a la estación de servicio para llenar el tanque de gasolina. ______

c. ______ Manolo y Ramón fueron a la tienda de deportes, porque querían saber cuánto costaban los patines. ______

d. ______ Ramón habló con Claudia por el celular para ir al Bazar San Ángel. ______

e. ______ Ramón se compró una camiseta del Cruz Azul. ______

Realidades 2 Nombre Hora

Capítulo 3A Fecha **VIDEO**

Actividad 3

Circle the correct word that completes the following sentences.

1. Los cuatro amigos quieren ir al (cine/correo) a ver una película (romántica/de ciencia ficción).
2. Teresa no compró el champú (ayer/hoy), porque fue a (devolver/comprar) un libro a la biblioteca.
3. (Claudia/Teresa) compra pasta dental en la farmacia.
4. El correo (abre/cierra) a las cinco.
5. A Teresa se le olvidó (llenar el tanque/enviar la carta) esta mañana.
6. Manolo (compra/no compra) los patines en la tienda de equipo deportivo.
7. Teresa olvidó (enviar/comprar) un regalo para el cumpleaños de su (abuela/mamá).
8. Claudia y Teresa van a ver a Ramón y a Manolo en el (correo/Bazar San Ángel) porque (no está muy lejos/ está muy lejos) de allí.

Y, ¿qué más?

Actividad 4

Write four complete sentences that tell about things you and your friends do and places that you and your friends go to in your free time. Follow the model.

Modelo *Me gusta ir con mis amigos(as) a jugar a los bolos.*

Nombre ____________________ Hora ________

Fecha ____________________

AUDIO

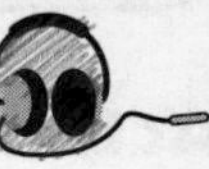

Actividad 5

Miguel is calling his friends to make plans for the day, but no one is available. Listen as each friend tells Miguel what he or she is doing, then write his or her name in the space under the picture that best illustrates the activity. You will hear each conversation twice.

____

____

____

____

____

____

Actividad 6

Felipe has been trying to catch up with his friend Moisés all day. As he asks people where they saw Moisés last, write the time and place each person mentions on the line beneath the appropriate picture. After you have heard everyone's answers, number the pictures chronologically, with **1** being the first place Moisés went and **8** being the last place Moisés went. You will hear each conversation twice.

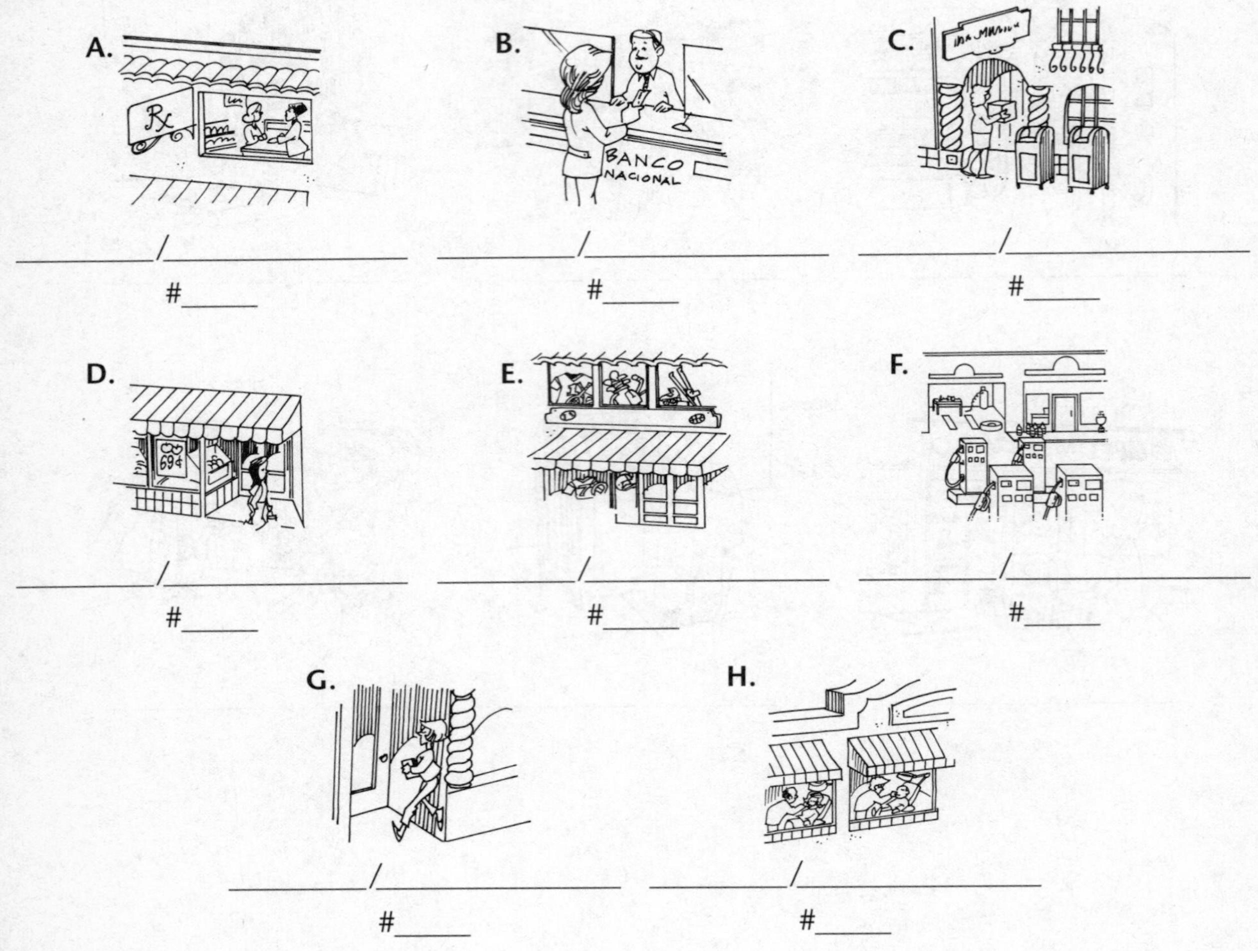

A. ____/____ #____
B. ____/____ #____
C. ____/____ #____
D. ____/____ #____
E. ____/____ #____
F. ____/____ #____
G. ____/____ #____
H. ____/____ #____

Actividad 7

Listen as you hear several people describe a moment when they saw someone who they thought was good-looking. After each statement, complete the sentence below with the correct location of the encounter. You will hear each statement twice.

1. Lo vio en ______________________.
2. La vio en ______________________.
3. Los vio en ______________________.
4. Las vio en ______________________.
5. La vio en ______________________.

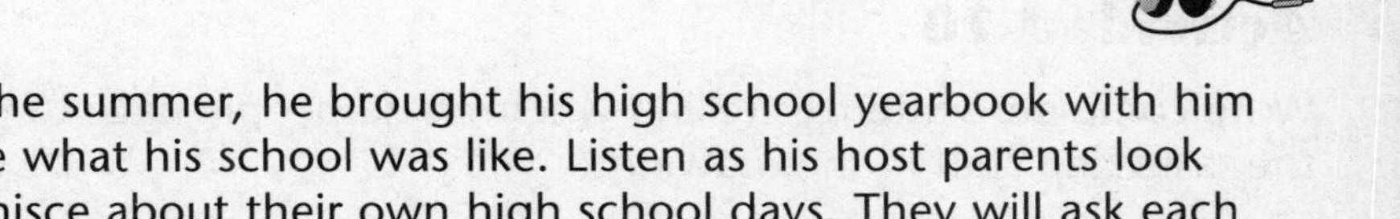

Realidades 2 | Nombre _______________ | Hora _______________

Capítulo 3A | Fecha _______________ | AUDIO

Actividad 8

When Eric went to Mexico for the summer, he brought his high school yearbook with him so that his host family could see what his school was like. Listen as his host parents look through his yearbook and reminisce about their own high school days. They will ask each other if they remember (**¿recuerdas?**) certain events from their past. Match their memories with the corresponding pictures. You will hear this conversation twice.

_______________ _______________ _______________

_______________ _______________

Actividad 9

Sometimes there just aren't enough hours in the day! Listen as each person tells a friend what he or she had to do yesterday but just wasn't able to. As you listen to each conversation, fill in the grid below with short phrases. You will hear each conversation twice.

	¿Qué tuvo que hacer la persona?	¿Por qué no pudo hacerlo?
1.		
2.		
3.		
4.		
5.		

Actividad 10

Write complete sentences telling where these people have to go today in order to accomplish the tasks depicted in the drawings.

1. Marta ____
____

2. Tito ____
____

3. Marisa y Laura ____
____

4. Juanito ____
____

Nombre ______ Hora ______

Fecha ______ **WRITING**

Actividad 11

Your little sister is curious about some of the things you have in your room. Explain what each item is, what you use it for, and when you use it, using complete sentences. Follow the model.

Modelo  *Son periódicos. Los leo todos los días después de terminar la tarea.*

1. ______

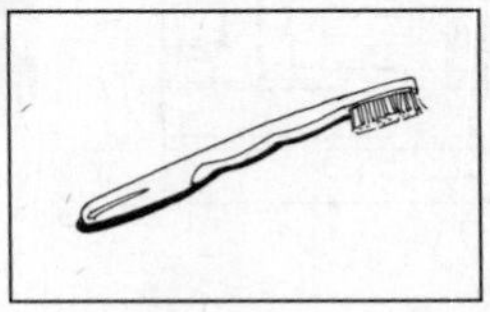

2. ______

3. ______

4. ______

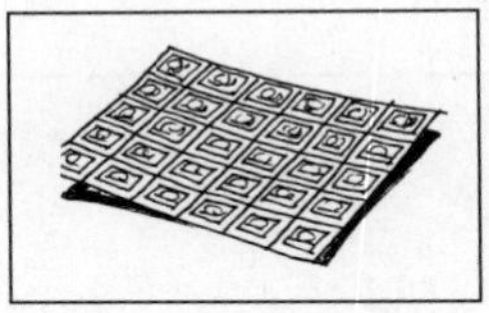

5. ______

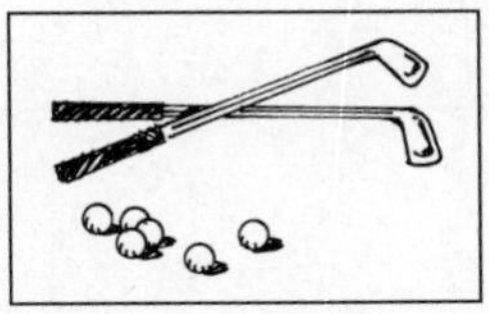

6. ______

7. ______

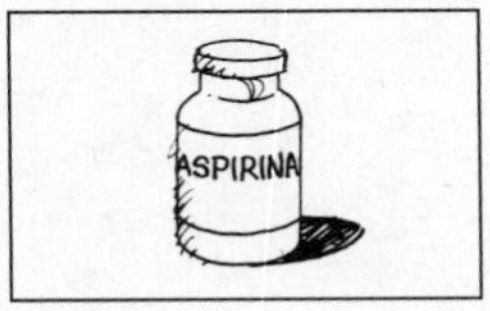

Actividad 12

You witnessed a bank robbery last night! Look at the pictures below that illustrate what happened, then write complete sentences to answer the police officer's questions that follow. Use the preterite forms of the verbs **ser** and/or **ir** in each sentence.

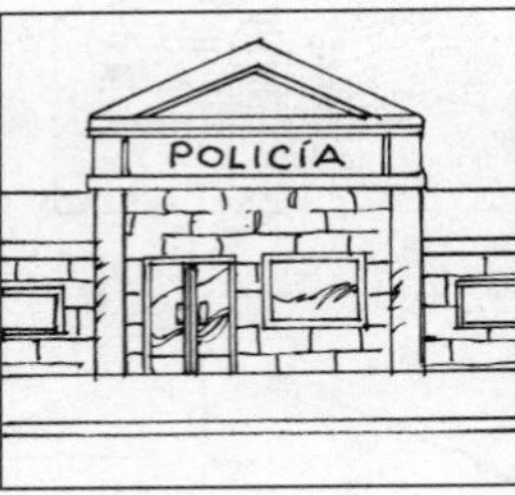

1. ¿Adónde fueron los ladrones (*thieves*) anoche?

   ___

2. ¿Adónde fuiste tú?

   ___

   ___

3. ¿Quiénes fueron los ladrones?

   ___

4. ¿Qué pasó después?

   ___

   ___

5. ¿Adónde fue los policías? ¿Y los ladrones?

   ___

   ___

Actividad 13

Your family just took a trip and you are going through your photos, reminiscing about the good and bad parts of the vacation. Write a caption for each picture below to describe what everyone did, where they went, what they were able to do there, etc.

Modelo *Juan Carlos y Dominga fueron a un hotel especial con club atlético. Estuvieron allí dos semanas. Pudieron jugar al tenis todos los días. Hicieron muchas actividades y tuvieron unas vacaciones fabulosas.*

1. ____

2. ____

3. ____

Realidades 2 Nombre ______ Hora ______

Capítulo 3B Fecha ______ VIDEO

Antes de ver el video

Actividad 1

How do you get to your Spanish classroom from the cafeteria? Write the directions on the lines below.

______

______

______

______

______

¿Comprendes?

Actividad 2

Who made each comment or asked each question below? Write the name of the corresponding character from the video in the space provided.

1. Vamos a tomar el metro. Claudia

2. Mira, aquí hay un banco… ¿Tienes prisa? Ramón

3. Hace mucho tiempo que no voy por allí. Pero te va a gustar. Manolo

4. ¿Estás seguro que sabes cómo llegar? Ramón

5. Espera… Esto es complicado. Mando

6. Claro, claro. Me estás poniendo nervioso. Yo sé por dónde vamos. Mando

7. Ya son las dos y cuarto. ¿Dónde estarán…? 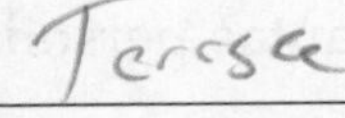

8. ¡Basta! Vamos a preguntar a alguien. Ramón

9. Oye, ¿podemos caminar un poco más despacio? 

10. Mira. Allí está el bazar. 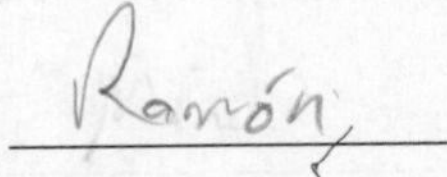

Nombre _______________ Hora _______________

Fecha _______________ VIDEO

Actividad 3

Manolo and Ramón want to meet up with Teresa and Claudia. Answer the questions below about the events that take place along the way.

1. ¿Cómo van Manolo y Ramón al Bazar San Ángel? ¿Y cómo llegan Claudia y Teresa allí?

2. ¿Quién llega al bazar primero? ¿Qué hacen allí?

3. ¿A cuántas personas pregunta Ramón sobre cómo se va al Bazar San Ángel?

Y, ¿qué más?

Actividad 4

You want to tell your friend how to get to the local YMCA, since she wants to play basketball. Use the following expressions to write directions.

doblas a (la derecha / la izquierda)
sigues (la avenida *nombre* / la calle *nombre*)
hasta (el primero / el segundo / el próximo) semáforo
sigues derecho por (esa avenida / esa calle) aproximadamente (dos / tres / cinco) millas
sigues esa avenida por (seis / siete / ocho) cuadras, hasta que veas el gimnasio

Estaciona el coche, y ¡a jugar al básquetbol!

Nombre ______________________ Hora ______________

Fecha ______________________ AUDIO

Actividad 5

Listen as people in a hotel call the front desk for help. As you listen to each conversation, match each caller to the spot on the map below by writing the number of the conversation in the corresponding circle. You will hear each conversation twice.

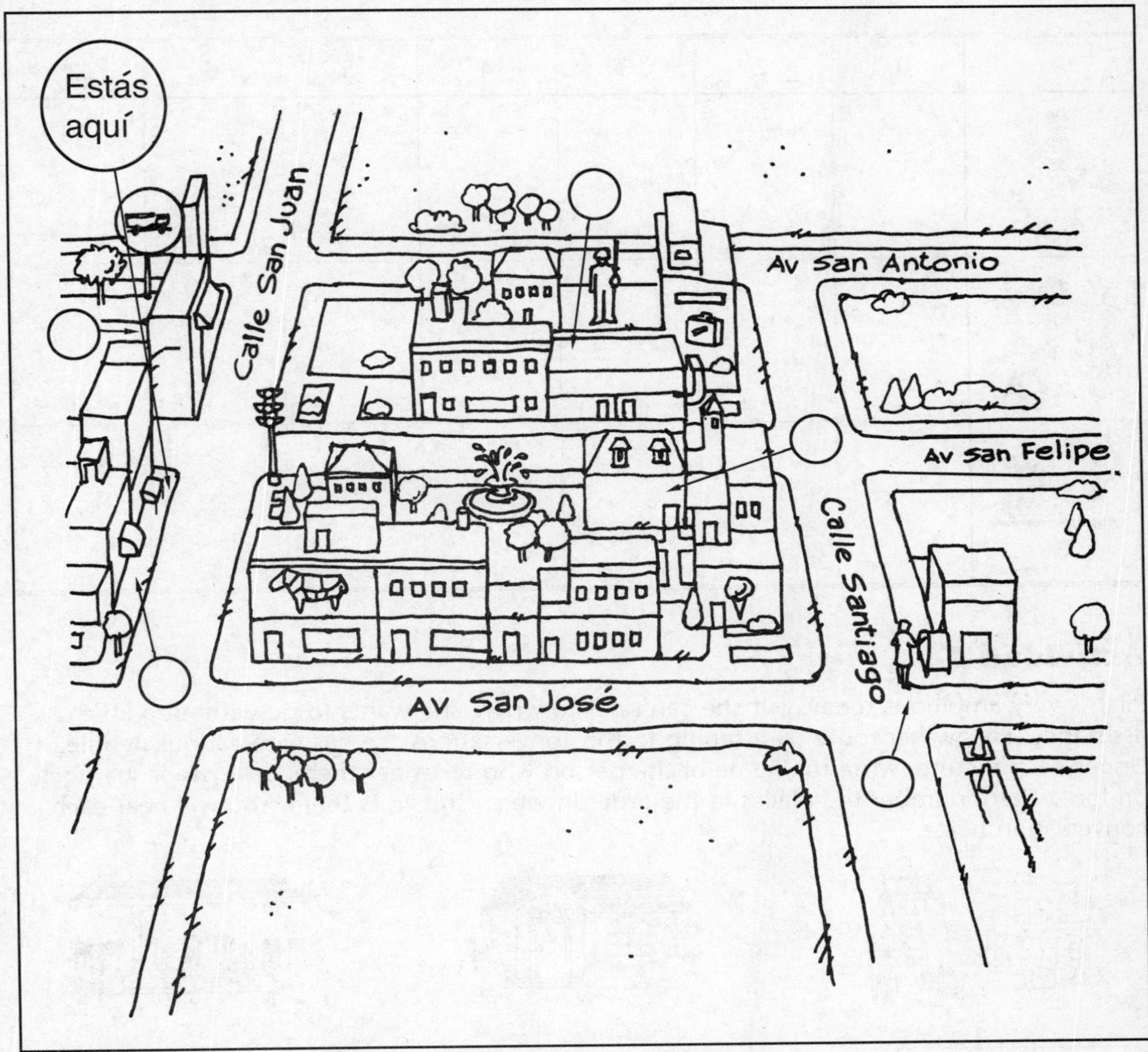

Actividad 6

Parents always seem to worry about their children as soon as they step out the door! As you listen to the parent's last piece of advice as each young person leaves, determine whether the young person is walking, riding a bicycle, or driving a car to his or her destination. Use the grid below to mark your answers. You will hear each piece of advice twice.

	1	2	3	4	5	6	7

Actividad 7

Pilar is very ambitious today, but she can't get to where she wants to go without a little assistance. Follow her route by listening to the conversations she has with various people. Under each picture, write the name of the person who takes her there, or **a pie** if she goes on foot. Then, number the places in the order in which she visits them. You will hear each conversation twice.

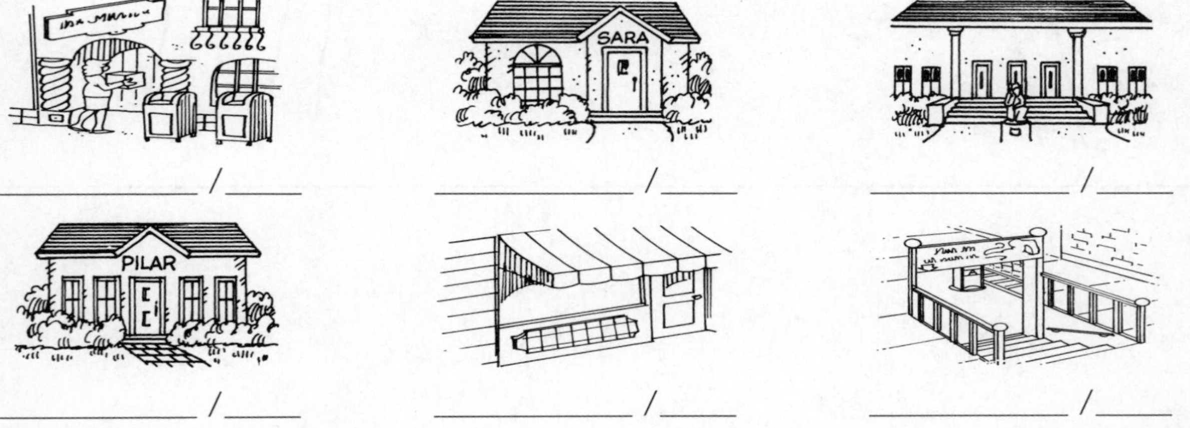

_____________ / _____ _____________ / _____ _____________ / _____

_____________ / _____ _____________ / _____ _____________ / _____

Nombre ______________________ Hora ______

Fecha ______________________

AUDIO

Actividad 8

Listen as an elementary school teacher gives instructions to several of her students during a field trip to a local park. Match each command to a picture of one of the children. In the blanks below, write in the letter of the corresponding picture. You will hear each set of instructions twice.

A.

B.
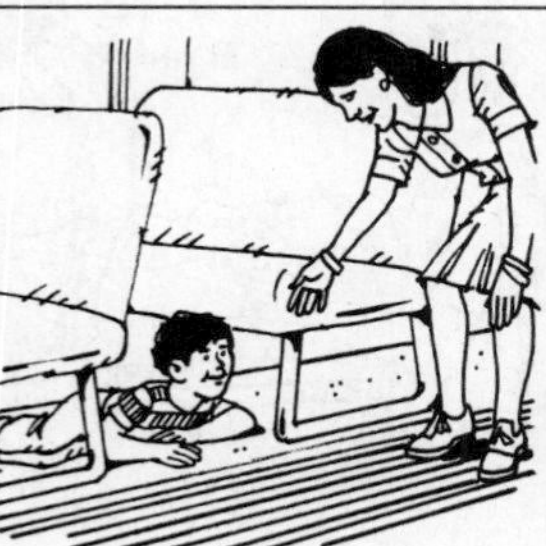

C.

D.

E.

F.

G.

H.

I.

J.

1. ______ 3. ______ 5. ______ 7. ______ 9. ______

2. ______ 4. ______ 6. ______ 8. ______ 10. ______

AUDIO

Actividad 9

The teacher in charge of after-school detention is going to be absent for a few days. Listen as she describes the students to the substitute teacher. Write the name of each student in the blank under the corresponding picture. You will hear each description twice.

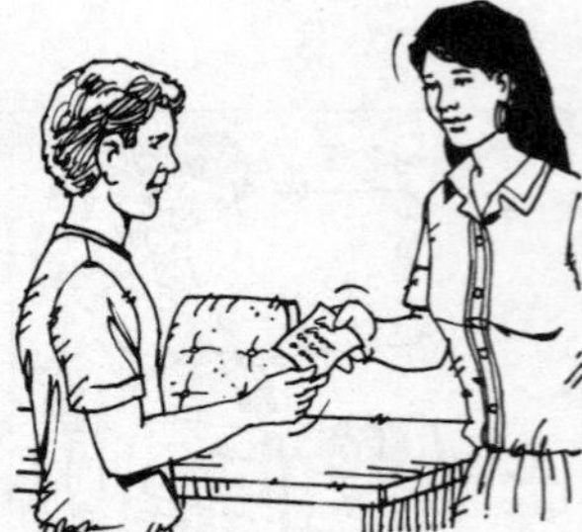

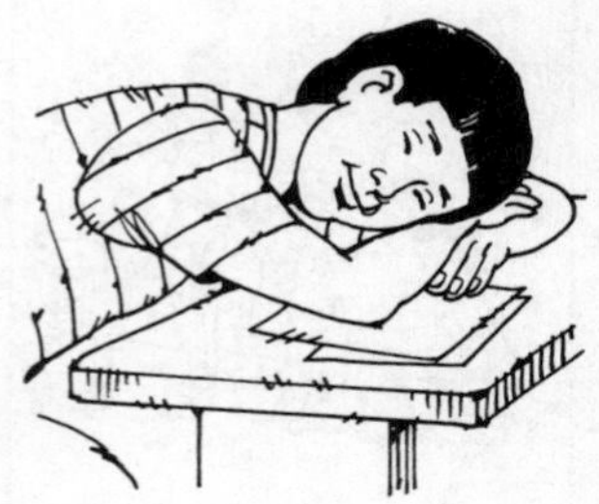

Actividad 10

You are giving directions to some friends about how to get to your cousin's house for a surprise party. Using the map below, tell them what landmarks they will pass on the way from each of their houses to the party.

1. Guillermo *Para llegar a la fiesta, vas a pasar por...*

2. Julieta *Para llegar a la fiesta, vas a pasar por...*

3. Marcos *Para llegar a la fiesta, vas a pasar por...*

Actividad 11

Your friends rely on you for help with various things. Write out your responses to the questions your friends ask you. You may answer in the affirmative or negative. Follow the model.

Modelo —¿Quieres hablar conmigo sobre la fiesta?
—*No, te hablé anoche*.

1. —¿En dónde vas a esperar a María y a Elena?
   —____________________.
2. —¿Vas a buscarme enfrente de la escuela?
   —____________________.
3. —¿Necesito llamar a Alejandro para saber dónde es la fiesta?
   —____________________.
4. —¿Alejandro nos invitó a ti y a mí a la fiesta?
   —____________________.
5. —¿Tengo que traer algo a la fiesta para ti?
   —____________________.
6. —¿Necesitas ayuda con algo?
   —____________________.
7. —¿Vienen tus tíos a la fiesta contigo?
   —____________________.
8. —¿Hablaste con ellos anoche?
   —____________________.
9. —¿Quieres ver a alguien en la fiesta?
   —____________________.
10. —¿Conoces a la familia Rodríguez?
    —____________________.

Actividad 12

As part of the interview process to become a camp counselor, you are asked to describe to the head counselor what you would tell kids to do in certain situations. Look at each drawing and write two affirmative **tú** commands for each, based on the hints provided. Include at least one of the following verbs each time: **poner, tener, decir, salir, venir, descansar, jugar, quedarse, hacer, ir,** and **ser.**

1. ve una serpiente (*snake*)

2. acaba de comer

3. no quiere participar

4. está enferma

5. tiene frío

6. no quiere hacer sus quehaceres

Realidades 2

Capítulo 3B

Nombre _______________ Hora _______________

Fecha _______________ **WRITING**

Actividad 13

You are keeping a journal of things that happen throughout the day. Look at each picture, and write a complete sentence to tell what time it is and what the people are doing at the moment. Follow the model.

Modelo Pablo

Son las dos y diez y Pablo está pidiéndole ayuda a la profesora.

1. **Mónica**

____.

2. **Jorge**

____.

3. **Yo**

____.

4. **Nosotros**

____.

5. **Tú**

____.

6. **La señora Vargas**

____.

Realidades 2 Nombre ____________________ Hora ________

Capítulo 4A Fecha ____________________ **VIDEO**

Antes de ver el video

Actividad 1

What were you like when you were younger? Think of several words that describe you. Then, use them in sentences about yourself. One has been done for you.

Palabras descriptivas	Oración sobre mí
generoso(a)	*Era muy generoso(a) con mis hermanos pequeños.*
	Era
	Era
	Era

¿Comprendes?

Actividad 2

Do you remember the conversations from the video about Ana as a little girl? Fill in the blanks below with the words that describe Ana in each of the scenes shown.

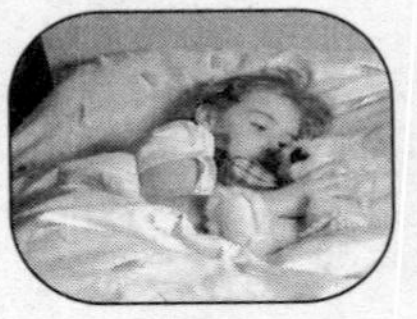

1. ¿Cómo era Ana de niña?
   Era muy ____________________.

2. ¿Qué dice Ignacio de Ana?
   Ignacio dice que era ____________________.

3. Según su mamá, ¿Ana era ____________________ de niña?
   No, por lo general era muy ____________________ y muy bien ____________________.

4. ¿Ana era siempre bien educada de niña?
   No, a veces era un poquito ____________________.

Realidades 2 Nombre Hora

Capítulo 4A Fecha

VIDEO

Actividad 3

All of the following sentences contain incorrect information. Rewrite each sentence to match what you learned in the video.

1. Ana, Elena e Ignacio trabajan en un proyecto para la clase de matemáticas.

2. De niña, Ana no tenía un juguete favorito.

3. Ana solamente tenía un animal de peluche, su oso.

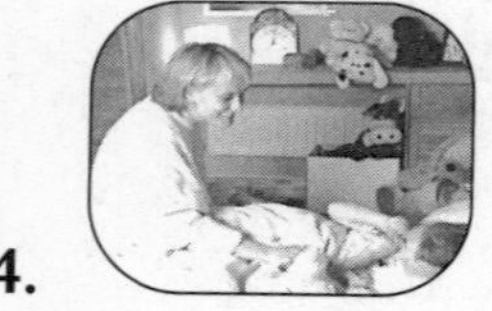

4. De niña, Ana siempre se levantaba tarde.

5. Elena cree que Ignacio siempre obedecía a sus padres y que siempre decía la verdad.

VIDEO

Y, ¿qué más?

Actividad 4

Draw a family tree of your immediate family. Next to each person, write a word to describe him or her. Then, write three sentences about your favorite relatives.

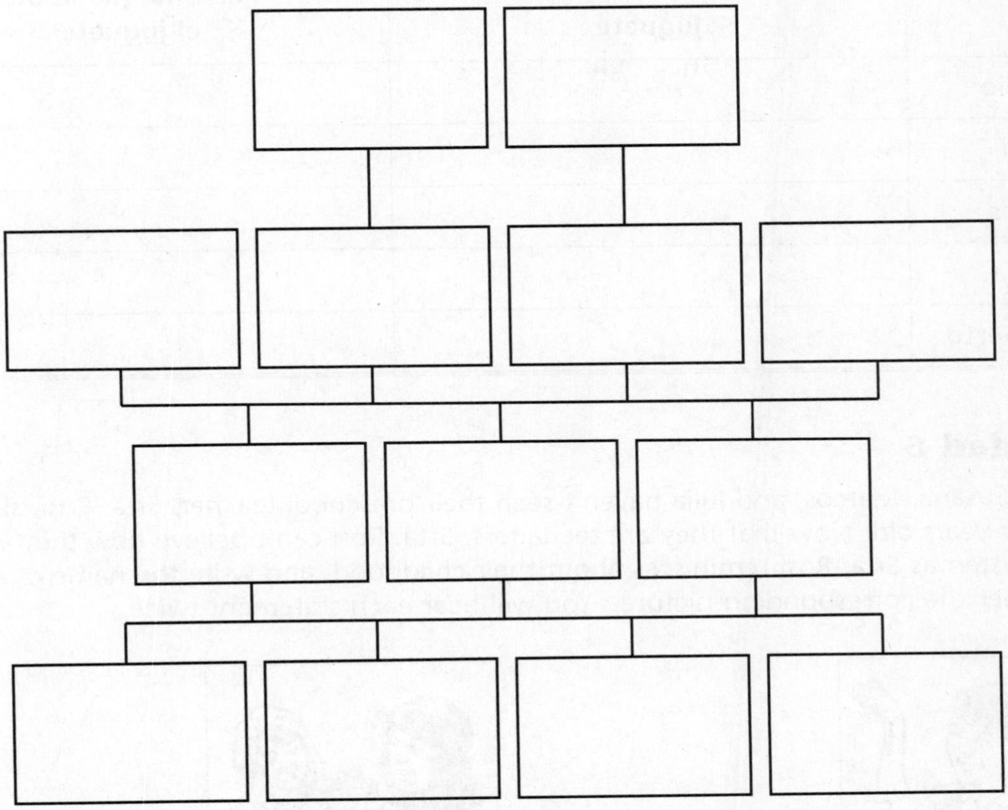

Actividad 5

Do you remember your favorite childhood toy? Listen as each of the following people describes a favorite childhood toy. In the grid below, write what each person's favorite toy was and who gave the toy to him or her. You will hear each set of statements twice.

	Juguete	Persona que le dio el juguete
Rogelio		
Marta		
Andrés		
Lorena		
Humberto		

Actividad 6

Ricardo, Susana, Marcos, and Julia haven't seen their preschool teacher, Srta. Rosi, since they were four years old. Now that they are teenagers, Srta. Rosi can't believe how they've grown. Listen as Srta. Rosi reminisces about their childhood, and write the name of each child under the corresponding picture. You will hear each statement twice.

______

______

______

______

Realidades 2 | Nombre ____ | Hora ____

Capítulo 4A | Fecha ____ | AUDIO

Actividad 7

Listen as Patricia listens to her favorite popular radio show **"Yo no lo sabía"** to find out things that she didn't know about some of her favorite movie and TV personalities. Match what you hear the DJ say about her favorite celebrities to the pictures below. Write the number of each piece of gossip underneath the picture it refers to. You will hear each piece of gossip twice.

____

____

____

____

____

____

____

____

Actividad 8

Listen as adults recall their childhood and how they used to role-play having different kinds of jobs when they grew up. Write the number of each description under the picture of the corresponding profession each person imagined as a child. You will hear each description twice.

Nombre ______________________ Hora __________

Fecha ______________________

AUDIO

Actividad 9

There are no gift tags on the Christmas gifts that the Rodríguez family received from their friend Gonzalo. Sr. Rodríguez has to call him on the phone to find out which gift goes to whom. Complete the sentences below to describe what Gonzalo gave to each person. For example, you might write, "**Gonzalo *le* dio unos aretes a *la abuela*.**" You will hear this conversation twice.

1. Gonzalo _____ dio unos boletos de avión a ____________________.
2. Gonzalo _____ dio su colección de tarjetas de béisbol a ____________________.
3. Gonzalo _____ dio dinero en efectivo a ____________________.
4. Gonzalo _____ dio unos zapatos de golf a ____________________.
5. Gonzalo _____ dio una colección de monedas al ____________________.

Actividad 10

Look at the scenes of children playing at a day care center. Then, write a sentence to tell what each child is doing.

1. Mario ________________.
2. Estela ________________.
3. Javier y Julia ________________.

4. Ricardo ________________.
5. Sandra y Beto ________________.
6. Susana ________________.

Realidades 2 | Nombre ______ Hora ______

Capítulo 4A | Fecha ______ **WRITING**

Actividad 11

You are at your best friend's family reunion, and all of the relatives are reminiscing about their childhood. Look at the pictures and tell what everyone did as children. Follow the model.

Modelo ¿Qué hacía el abuelito?

El abuelito pescaba con su padre ______.

1. ¿Qué hacía la tía Ramona?

______.

2. ¿Qué hacía el padre?

______.

3. ¿Qué hacían tú y tu abuela?

______.

4. ¿Qué hacían los tíos?

______.

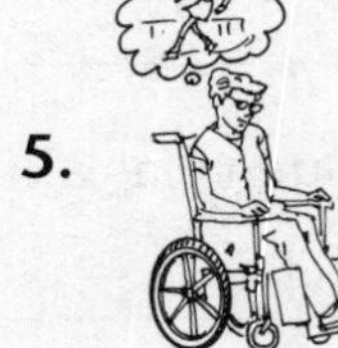

5. ¿Qué hacía la abuela?

______.

6. ¿Y tú? ¿Qué hacías de niño?

______.

Actividad 12

Read the sentences that tell what the people below used to do when they were your age. Then, answer the questions that follow in complete sentences. Follow the model.

Modelo Cuando Juliana y María tenían 14 años, ellas contaban muchos chistes *(jokes)*. Se reían mucho y les gustaba ver las comedias en el cine.

¿Cómo eran las chicas? *Ellas eran cómicas* .

¿Adónde iban para ver las comedias? *Iban al cine* .

1. Cuando Marta tenía 16 años, ella trabajaba mucho. Estudiaba y leía. También le gustaba ver programas educativos en la tele todos los días.

   ¿Cómo era Marta? ______________________.

   ¿Qué veía todos los días? ______________________

   ______________________.

2. Cuando Óscar y Humberto tenían 14 años, practicaban muchos deportes. En el invierno practicaban el hockey en la calle y en la primavera jugaban al básquetbol en el gimnasio.

   ¿Cómo eran los chicos? ______________________.

   ¿Adónde iban para practicar sus deportes? ______________________

   ______________________.

3. Cuando nosotros teníamos 15 años, nos gustaba pintar y dibujar. También nos encantaba mirar obras de arte de artistas famosos como Dalí y Picasso en el museo.

   ¿Cómo éramos? ______________________.

   ¿Adónde íbamos y qué veíamos allí? ______________________

   ______________________.

4. ¿Y tú? ¿Qué hacías cuando eras niño(a)? ¿Cómo eras? ¿Adónde ibas? ¿Qué veías allí?

   ____

   ____

   ____

   ______________________.

Realidades 2 | Nombre | Hora

Capítulo 4A | Fecha | **WRITING**

Actividad 13

A. Look at each drawing of people giving gifts to each other. Write a complete sentence to describe what people gave each other. Follow the model.

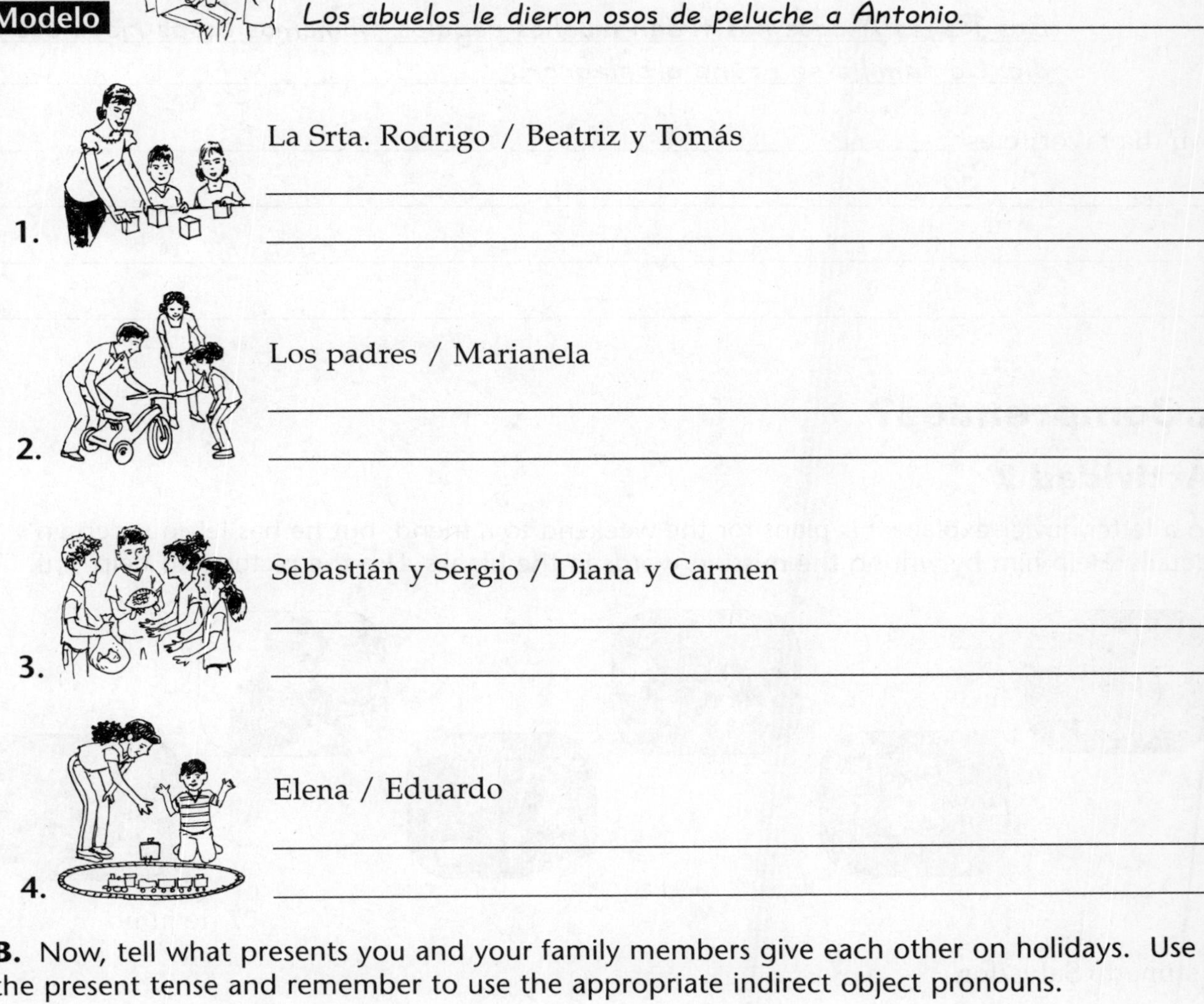

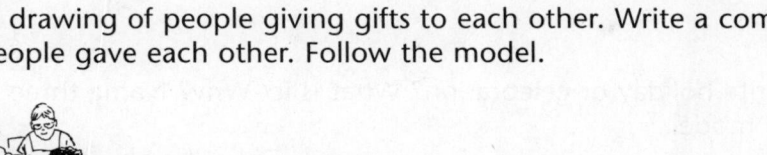

Modelo Los abuelos / Antonio

Los abuelos le dieron osos de peluche a Antonio.

1. La Srta. Rodrigo / Beatriz y Tomás

2. Los padres / Marianela

3. Sebastián y Sergio / Diana y Carmen

4. Elena / Eduardo

B. Now, tell what presents you and your family members give each other on holidays. Use the present tense and remember to use the appropriate indirect object pronouns.

Antes de ver el video

Actividad 1

Do you have a favorite holiday or celebration? What is it? Why? Name three special things about it. Follow the model.

Modelo Mi día favorito es *el Día de los tres Reyes Magos.*
Los Reyes Magos nos traen muchos regalos. Comemos cosas ricas ese día. La familia se reúne a celebrar.

Mi día favorito es ______________________________

____

____

____

¿Comprendes?

Actividad 2

In a letter, Javier explains his plans for the weekend to a friend, but he has left out certain details. Help him by writing the missing words in the blanks. Use the pictures to help you.

27 de junio

Estimado Salvador,

Este fin de semana me voy con mi amigo Ignacio al pueblo de su madre, ____________________. Ignacio me dice que siempre llueve y necesitamos llevar un paraguas. Durante el fin de semana, ellos celebran la ____________________. De niño, él siempre pasaba los veranos allá. Todos los años, la fiesta comienza con un ________________. Hay bailes y músicos, y ellos tocan instrumentos ________________ y ______________. Algunos de los instrumentos son el txistu y el tamboril. El txistu es una palabra vasca para una ______________. Ignacio sabe tocar el txistu, pero no sabe hablar __________, como sus ______________. Luego todos se reúnen en la iglesia, donde celebran una misa en español y en vasco. Esto es una ______________. Bueno, Salvador, te cuento más al regresar.

Tu amigo, *Javier*

Actividad 3

Match each word or phrase on the left with its corresponding sentence on the right.

1. ______ la fiesta de San Pedro
2. ______ txistu

3. ______ txistorra

4. ______ ropa típica

5. ______ una boina
6. ______ vasco

7. ______ desfile
8. ______ antiguos
9. ______ paraguas

a. En la maleta pongo una camisa blanca, un pañuelo rojo y una boina roja.

b. Comienza en la mañana, cuando todos nos reunimos en esta marcha ordenada, generalmente para celebrar la fiesta.

c. Mi abuelo me enseñó a tocar este instrumento cuando yo era pequeño.

d. Este idioma lo hablan los abuelos de Ignacio.

e. Me llevo esto para la lluvia porque siempre llueve, pero no importa.

f. Los músicos tocan instrumentos típicos y muy viejos, o ____________.

g. Javier no tiene una gorra redonda, o un tipo de sombrero típico.

h. Tienen hambre, y quieren comer este tipo de salchicha.

i. Esta fiesta siempre se celebra el 29 de junio.

Y, ¿qué más?

Actividad 4

Your cousin invited you this past weekend to spend it with his/her family, for a special celebration. Where did you go and what did you do? In a simple paragraph, explain your weekend. Use your imagination and follow the model.

Modelo *El fin de semana pasado fui a la casa de mi primo favorito, para celebrar su cumpleaños. La fiesta fue en un centro comercial. Allí jugamos a los bolos. Luego comimos un pastel de chocolate y bebimos refrescos. También cantamos y bailamos mucho. Finalmente, regresamos a su casa y dormí allá. Al día siguiente, mis padres volvieron por mí.*

Actividad 5

Mrs. Lena is taking her third grade class to visit a group of senior citizens tomorrow. In order to make sure that all the children behave well at the Senior Center, she uses puppets named **Marco el malo** and **Bruno el bueno** to illustrate good and bad manners. Listen as she describes what each puppet does, and decide if the actions are most likely those of **Marco el malo** or **Bruno el bueno.** Put an X in the appropriate box in the grid below. You will hear this conversation twice.

	1	2	3	4	5	6	7	8

Actividad 6

Listen as four people talk about their favorite time to spend with their families. Write the number of the description under the corresponding picture. You will hear each description twice.

______

______

______

______

Realidades 2 | Nombre _______________ | Hora _______

Capítulo 4B | Fecha _______________ | **AUDIO**

Actividad 7

When José Ignacio's mother returned from grocery shopping, she was shocked by some of the things her children and their friends were doing! Listen as she later tells José Ignacio's father what was going on when she got home. Based on what she says, fill in the grid below to tell how they were behaving. You will hear each set of statements twice.

	1	2	3	4	5	6
Se portaban bien						
Se portaban mal						

Actividad 8

Some best friends like to do everything together, while others prefer to spend some time apart. Listen as some teenagers talk about whether they prefer to do certain things separately or together. Then, put an X in the appropriate box in the grid. You will hear each set of statements twice.

	1	2	3	4	5	6	7
Juntos (*together*)							
Solo							

Realidades 

Capítulo 4B

Nombre ______________________ Hora ________

Fecha ______________________

AUDIO

Actividad 9

Listen as parents tell their children about their childhood memories of family celebrations and traditions. As you listen, match each conversation to the pictures below by writing the number of the conversation under the appropriate picture. You will hear each conversation twice.

____

____

____

____

____

Nombre ______ Hora ______

Fecha ______ **WRITING**

Actividad 10

Josephine is an exchange student in Spain and wants to make sure she acts appropriately when greeting people. Help her by answering her questions about what people tend to do in the situations she describes. Follow the model.

Modelo ¿Qué hago para saludar a una persona que conozco bien?
Uds. se besan o se abrazan para saludarse.

1. ¿Qué hago cuando encuentro a una persona que no veo con frecuencia?

______

2. ¿Qué digo cuando una persona se casa o se gradúa de la universidad?

______

3. ¿Qué hago cuando conozco a una persona por primera vez?

______

4. ¿Qué hago cuando salgo de un lugar o de la casa por la mañana?

______

5. ¿Qué hago cuando no veo a una amiga por mucho tiempo y quiero verla?

______

6. ¿Qué hago cuando paso a una persona a quien no conozco en la calle?

______

Actividad 11

Your friends had a very eventful weekend. Look at the illustrations of what happened, and write a brief description of what the people in the scene were doing and what happened to interrupt them. Follow the model.

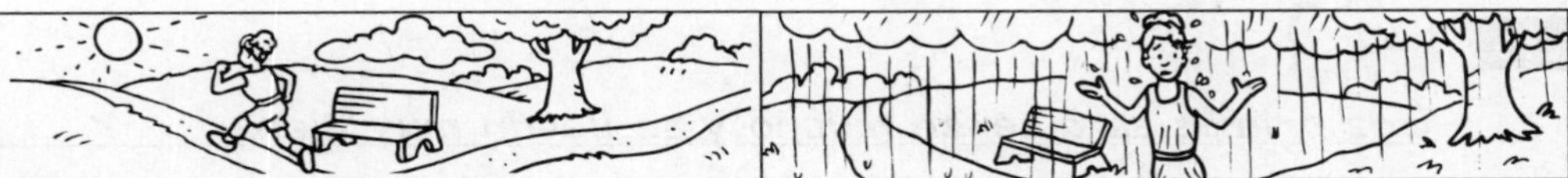

Mónica: *Hacía buen tiempo y Mónica estaba en el parque. Corría cuando empezó a llover.*

1. 

Pancho y Patricia: ______________________________

____

2. 

Nosotras: ______________________________

____

3. 

Ellos: ______________________________

____

4. 

Yo: ______________________________

____

WRITING

Actividad 12

A. Lolis and Teresa are cousins who live quite far away from each other. Look at the pictures below and write complete sentences about what they do. Follow the model.

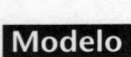

Modelo *Las primas se quieren mucho y se llevan muy bien.*

1. 

____

2. 

____

3. 

____

4. 

____

5.

____

B. Now, write about a cousin or other relative you like who lives far away. Follow the model.

Modelo *Mi prima Cristina y yo nos vemos una vez cada dos años.*

____

____

____

Realidades 2 Nombre _______ Hora _______

Capítulo 4B Fecha _______ **WRITING**

Actividad 13

Pablo's family has just returned from a family reunion and he is writing in his diary about the day's events.

A. First, look at the picture of the party and write several sentences to describe the scene.

____

____

____

____

B. Next, tell what everyone at the party did when they were first reunited.

____

____

____

C. Finally, help Pablo write his diary entry using the phrases that you wrote above and any connecting words you may need to make your paragraph smooth.

Querido diario:

Hoy fui a la reunión de mi familia en San Juan.

____

____

____

____

____

____

____

Realidades 2 | Nombre ______ | Hora ______

Capítulo 5A | Fecha ______ | VIDEO

Antes de ver el video

Actividad 1

In this video, you are going to see part of a television newscast. Fill out the survey below about the news program that you normally watch at home.

Nombre del noticiero ______

Canal ______

Horario ______

¿Recuerdas el nombre de algún reportero (alguna reportera)? ______

______

¿Te gusta más ver los deportes? ¿las noticias? ¿el pronóstico del tiempo (*weather forecast*)?

¿Por qué te gusta esa sección más? ______

______

¿Comprendes?

Actividad 2

Read the following parts of the plot. Then, put them in the order in which they occurred. Write **1** for the first thing that happened and **7** for the last thing that happened.

______ Raúl y Tomás ven el noticiero en la tele.

______ Raúl y Tomás hablan con la reportera.

______ Comienza el incendio.

______ Ocurre la explosión.

______ El bombero habla con la reportera.

______ Un vecino ve el humo.

______ Vienen los paramédicos.

Actividad 3

In the video, Raúl and Tomás are watching TV when they hear the news about a fire. What happens afterwards? Answer the following questions in order to better understand the plot.

1. ¿En dónde ocurre el incendio?

2. ¿Quién es Laura Martínez? ¿Por qué está en el sitio del incendio?

3. ¿Cómo comenzó el incendio?

4. ¿Quién estaba en la casa cuando ocurrió el incendio?

5. ¿Quiénes vinieron para ayudar a rescatarlos?

6. ¿Por qué la reportera termina rápido la entrevista con Raúl y Tomás?

Realidades 2 Nombre _______________ Hora _______

Capítulo 5A Fecha _______________ VIDEO

Y, ¿qué más?

Actividad 4

Imagine that you are a reporter for a television newscast and you have to report on something that happened in your high school. Write a reporting script about a real or imaginary event at your high school. Follow the model.

Modelo *Les habla Lucía Pacheco, del canal 8. Estamos en el colegio Spring, donde un grupo de estudiantes de noveno grado está lavando coches. El dinero que reciben es para pagar un viaje a San Antonio, organizado por la profesora de historia, la Sra. Martínez. El viaje está planeado para el próximo mes de marzo. Esto es todo por ahora. Lucía Pacheco, desde el colegio Spring, para el canal 8.*

Actividad 5

Listen as these radio announcers break into regular programming to report emergency situations that have occurred. Match each radio report with one of the pictures below to indicate what type of emergency or crisis situation each was. Then, try to answer the bonus question in the last column for each news report. You will hear each report twice.

						Bonus Question
1						Según sus vecinos, ¿qué es el Sr. Morales?
2						¿Qué fue(ron) destruido(s)?
3						¿Qué necesita la gente?
4						¿Cómo puede ir la gente de un lugar a otro?
5						¿Quién es Gabriel?

Realidades 2 Nombre ________ Hora ________

Capítulo 5A Fecha ________ **AUDIO**

Actividad 6

As Ernesto is driving home from work, he turns on the radio and starts to scan for his favorite type of music. Each time he finds a station, a reporter is in the middle of the evening news report. As you listen, write the number of the excerpt under the corresponding picture. You will hear each report twice.

Actividad 7

A local jewelry store manager is holding a contest for young couples who purchase their wedding rings in his store. If there is bad weather on their wedding day, the manager promises to refund the couple the cost of their rings! Listen as each couple describes their wedding day. Which couples would qualify for a refund? Mark your answers in the grid below. You will hear each description twice.

	1	2	3	4	5	6
Qualify						
Do not qualify						

Actividad 8

When it comes to the news, some people prefer to listen to the radio while others would rather read the newspaper. Listen to people talk about recent events. Determine whether they HEARD about it on the radio or if they READ about it in the newspaper. Place a check mark in the appropriate row of the grid. You will hear each conversation twice.

	1	2	3	4	5

Actividad 9

Your teacher has asked you to listen to the news on a Spanish-speaking radio station. First, read the questions below. Then, listen to a news report of a hurricane that occurred yesterday in a small town near San Juan. As you listen to the story, circle the correct answers below. Your teacher might ask you to write a summary of the news story based on your answers. You will hear the report twice.

1. ¿Quién es Carmen Dominó?
   a. Una reportera. b. Una bombera. c. Una heroína.
2. ¿Qué es Felipe?
   a. Un noticiero. b. Un huracán. c. Un pueblo.
3. ¿Qué hacían muchas personas cuando el huracán llegó?
   a. Escuchaban la radio. b. Leían. c. Dormían.
4. ¿Qué pasó en Dorado a causa del huracán?
   a. Había mucha comida. b. Muchos vecinos perdieron sus casas.
   c. Había muchos muebles.
5. ¿Quiénes fueron los héroes de Dorado?
   a. Los médicos. b. Los reporteros. c. Los bomberos.

Realidades 2 Nombre ______ Hora ______

Capítulo 5A Fecha ______ **WRITING**

Actividad 10

You just finished watching the evening news. Under each news category below, write a short summary of the stories of the day by looking at each picture and using appropriate vocabulary. The first one has been started for you.

1. El tiempo

Hoy pasó un gran huracán por las islas de Venezuela.

______

______

______

______

2. La ciudad

______

______

______

______

3. Una ocurrencia heroica

______

______

______

______

Actividad 11

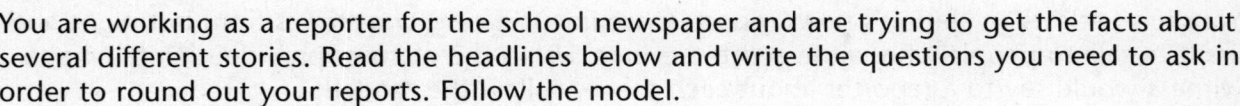

You are working as a reporter for the school newspaper and are trying to get the facts about several different stories. Read the headlines below and write the questions you need to ask in order to round out your reports. Follow the model.

Modelo **EL EQUIPO DE BÁSQUETBOL GANÓ AYER**

¿Qué hora era cuando empezó el partido?

¿Quién y cómo era el otro equipo?

¿Cómo se sentía el equipo de nuestra escuela cuando ganó?

1. **NUESTRA ESCUELA #2 EN EL CONCURSO DE MATEMÁTICAS**

2. **EL PRINCIPAL DECLARÓ: ¡NO SE PERMITE LLEVAR PANTALONES CORTOS!**

3. **¡EL BAILE DE LA ESCUELA UN ÉXITO!**

4. **JONES Y RULFO GANARON LAS ELECCIONES**

5. **¡INCENDIO EN LA CAFETERÍA!**

Actividad 12

Your local television station's news reporters are investigating two stories from last night and want to talk to people who witnessed the events. Using the pictures provided, write what a witness would say to a reporter about each scene. Follow the model.

Modelo La señora Alfonso *oyó los perros ladrando (barking)*.

1. Enrique y Roberto __________.
2. El incendio __________.
3. Tú __________.
4. Ignacio __________.
5. El ladrón (*robber*) __________.
6. Marisol y yo __________.
7. Yo __________.

Actividad 13

A. You want to write a mystery story about a crime that took place in a small town. In order to start developing the plot, answer the questions below using your imagination.

1. ¿Qué hora era y dónde estabas? ______
2. ¿Qué era el ruido (*noise*) que oíste? ______
3. ¿Cómo era el hombre que viste? ¿Qué hizo? ______
4. ¿Qué tenía en su mochila? ______
5. ¿Qué hora era cuando empezó el incendio? ______
6. ¿A qué hora llegaron los bomberos? ______
7. ¿Qué hiciste después? ______

B. Now, organize your answers into a short description of the plot of your story. You may wish to add details or connecting words to make it flow well. Be creative!

Realidades 2 Nombre ________ Hora ________

Capítulo 5B Fecha ________ VIDEO

Antes de ver el video

Actividad 1

When do you need to stay in bed because you are sick, and when do you need to go to the hospital? Write three examples for each. The first ones have been done for you.

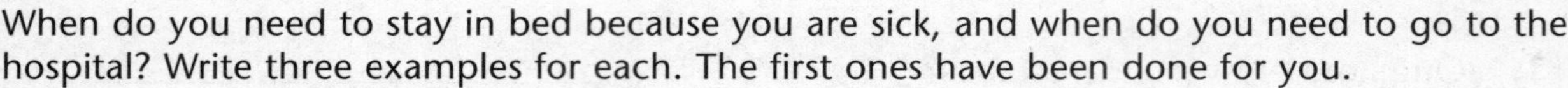

¿Cuándo me quedo en cama?	¿Cuándo voy al hospital?
Cuando tengo un dolor de cabeza muy fuerte	*Cuando me lastimo el brazo*

¿Comprendes?

Actividad 2

Identify the speaker of each of the following quotes from the video.

1. "Si no hay un terremoto él no se despierta ..." ________
2. "¡Qué lástima! ... ¿Y Tomás?" ________
3. "¡Ay, Dios mío!" ________
4. "¿Qué pasó entonces?" ________
5. "¡Pobre Tomás!" ________
6. "¡El pobrecito soy yo!" ________
7. "¡No debes despertarte a las tres de la mañana!" ________
8. "¿Por qué no me dijeron nada?" ________

Actividad 3

Look at each video scene and write one or two complete sentences to tell what is happening.

1. ____

____

2.

3.

4.

5.

6.

Y, ¿qué más?

Actividad 4

Have you ever had a silly accident? What happened? Answer the questions about your accident or the accident of someone you know.

1. ¿Qué hacías cuando ocurrió el accidente?

2. ¿Te lastimaste algo?

3. ¿Fuiste a la sala de emergencia? ¿Qué pasó?

Nombre ______________________ Hora ________

Fecha ______________________

AUDIO

Actividad 5

Your friend Juan Luis just spent his first day as a volunteer in the local hospital's emergency room. Listen as he tells his parents what happened. Write the number of the description in the corresponding circle in the picture below. You will hear each description twice.

Sala de emergencia

Actividad 6

Listen as several teenagers talk about what happened when they were injured recently. Match what each describes to one of the pictures below. Write the corresponding letter in the blanks below. You will hear each description twice.

A.
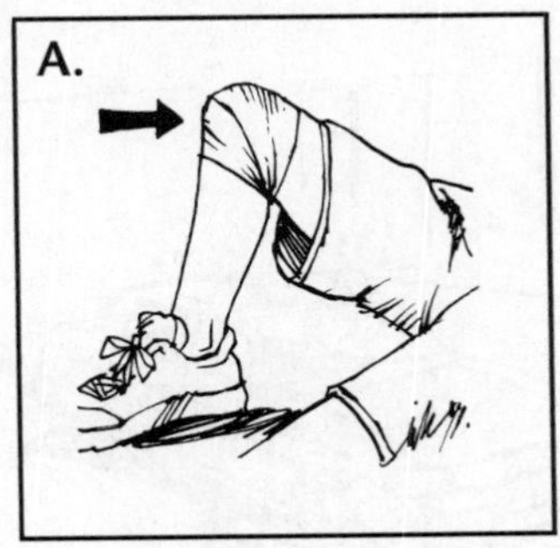

B.
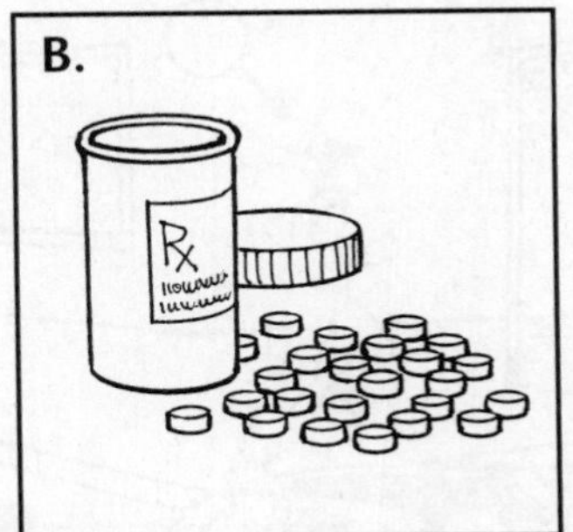

C.
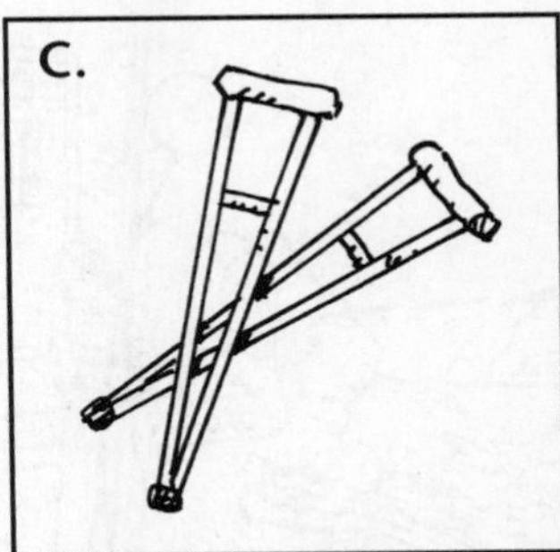

D.
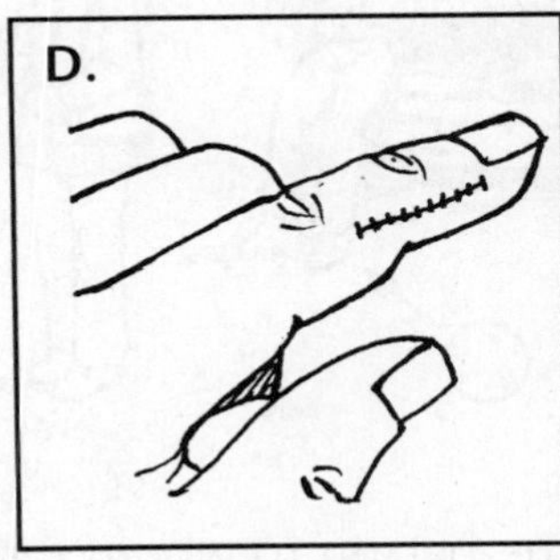

E.
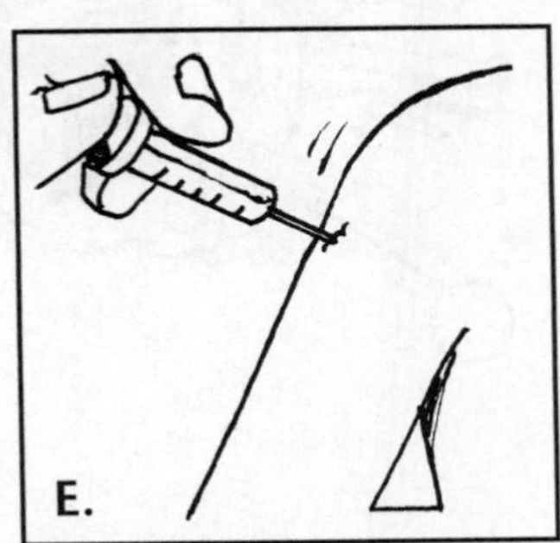

1. ______ 2. ______ 3. ______ 4. ______ 5. ______

Actividad 7

A popular **telenovela** added a new character to the cast of people who work at the fictitious hospital in the show. The character, Lola Loca, was added to give humor to the show. Many of the things she does are illogical and silly. Just listen to the things she did last week on the show! Fill in the grid below to show how you would categorize her actions. You will hear each statement twice.

	1	2	3	4	5	6	7	8
Lógico								
Ilógico								

Actividad 8

A group of friends was recalling what each was doing when the police arrived at the scene of an accident. Write the number of the statement in the corresponding circle in the picture below. You will hear each statement twice.

Actividad 9

As a counselor at a boy's summer camp, Jorge is the person to whom the children report any accidents or injuries. Listen as children run to Jorge and tell him what campers were doing when a recent injury occurred. Take notes in the grid below about what happened to each child. You will hear each set of statements twice.

Nombre del niño	¿Qué estaba haciendo el niño?	¿Qué se lastimó?
Jaime		
Luis		
Cristóbal		
Óscar		
Félix		

Actividad 10

The school nurse is explaining to some students situations in which they might need the medical treatments pictured below. Write what you might say about each treatment. Follow the model.

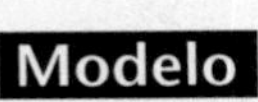

Necesitas un yeso cuando te caes de la escalera y te rompes la pierna.

1. ______________________________

2. ______________________________

3. ______________________________

4. ______________________________

5. ______________________________

6. ______________________________

7. ______________________________

Actividad 11

Carmela is writing in her diary after a busy day. Look at the pictures below of what she and her friends did, and write short diary entries based on each one. Follow the model.

Modelo Javier *le dijo la verdad a su padre. No pudo mentirle a su papá.*

1. Mariel ______________________________

2. Elena y yo ______________________________

3. Mis hermanos ______________________________

4. Ayer yo ______________________________

5. El cartero ______________________________

6. A las nueve los estudiantes ______________________________

Realidades 2 | Nombre ______ | Hora ______

Capítulo 5B | Fecha ______ | **WRITING**

Actividad 12

On Friday the 13th, lots of people had bad luck. Tell what the people below were doing when something bad happened. Use the imperfect progressive tense and be creative. Follow the model.

Modelo Yo me torcí el tobillo.

Yo estaba corriendo en el parque y no vi el plátano en la calle. Me caí.

1. Marcos se rompió la pierna. ______
2. Luisa y su mamá chocaron con una bicicleta. ______
3. ¡Yo salí de la casa sin pantalones y sin mis llaves! ______
4. Tú te lastimaste la cabeza. ______
5. El camarero rompió todos los platos. ______
6. Nosotros tropezamos con los juguetes en el piso de la sala. ______
7. Paco y Ramón se cortaron los dedos. ______
8. Marta y yo nos enfermamos. ______
9. Yo choqué con otro estudiante en la escuela. ______
10. Tú te torciste la muñeca izquierda. ______

Realidades 2 | Nombre ____ | Hora ____

Capítulo 5B | Fecha ____ | **WRITING**

Actividad 13

Julieta is a girl who likes to do too many things at once. Last week, her hectic lifestyle finally caught up with her.

A. Look at the picture below and describe at least four activities Julieta was doing at the same time. Follow the model.

Modelo *Julieta estaba leyendo.*

1. ____
2. ____
3. ____
4. ____
5. ____

B. Now, think about a hectic day you or someone you know had recently. Write five sentences to tell what happened. Follow the model.

Modelo *Mi hermana Julia estaba caminando y comiendo cuando se cayó y se lastimó la cabeza.*

1. ____
2. ____
3. ____
4. ____
5. ____

Realidades 2 | Nombre ______ | Hora ______

Capítulo 6A | Fecha ______ | VIDEO

Antes de ver el video

Actividad 1

In this video you will hear an interview with a famous soccer player. Write six sentences the player might use to describe what happened in a recent game. Follow the model.

Modelo *El jugador metió un gol.*

1. ______
2. ______
3. ______
4. ______
5. ______
6. ______

¿Comprendes?

Actividad 2

Read the following statements about the video and decide whether they are **cierto** or **falso.** If the statement is true, write ***cierto.*** If it is **falso,** rewrite the statement to make it true.

1. Manolo y Ramón están viendo una entrevista en la tele.

______

2. Claudia tiene interés en la entrevista de Luis Campos.

______

3. Luis Campos es el mejor jugador de las Águilas del América.

______

4. Manolo y Ramón tienen planes para ir al partido de hoy.

______

5. Claudia sabe cómo pueden ver el partido en el estadio.

______

6. Manolo y Ramón no quieren ir con Claudia al estadio para ver el partido.

______

Actividad 3

Do you remember what happened in the video? Using the pictures to help you, summarize the video in your own words. Follow the model.

1

2

3

4

Modelo *Manolo y Ramón vieron una entrevista con "la Pantera", Luis Campos.*

1. ______________________________

____

2. ______________________________

____

3. ______________________________

____

4. ______________________________

____

Y, ¿qué más?

Actividad 4

If you were a reporter for the school newspaper, who would you interview? Why? Answer these questions. Then, write five questions you would ask during the interview. Follow the model.

Modelo *Voy a entrevistar a la presidenta del club de español. Quiero saber las actividades que planea para el semestre.*

____

____

____

____

____

VIDEO

Actividad 5

The popular radio program **"Nuestra comunidad"** is highlighting three successful young women from the local Spanish-speaking community. As you listen to parts of their interviews, use the pictures below to decide whether the young woman speaking is Laura, Flor, or Isabel. Then, write the name of the young woman in the corresponding space. You will hear each set of statements twice.

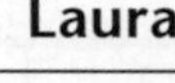

Laura	Flor	Isabel

1. ______ 3. ______ 5. ______ 7. ______
2. ______ 4. ______ 6. ______ 8. ______

Actividad 6

In the past few years there has been a growing interest in women's soccer. Listen as Don Balón interviews Eva Barca, a rising women's soccer star. As you hear the different segments of the interview, read the following statements and tell whether each is **cierto** or **falso.** You will hear each segment twice.

1. Eva Barca escucha el programa de Don Balón. **Cierto** **Falso**
2. Don Balón sólo entrevista a las mujeres. **Cierto** **Falso**
3. Las mujeres ganan más dinero que los hombres. **Cierto** **Falso**
4. Hay un muñeco de Eva Barca. **Cierto** **Falso**
5. Según Eva, no hay muñecos de los hombres jugadores. **Cierto** **Falso**
6. Según Eva, su entrenador grita demasiado. **Cierto** **Falso**
7. Según Eva, los aficionados son iguales para las dos ligas. **Cierto** **Falso**

Actividad 7

How do contestants spend their free time during the "**Señorita América del Sur**" beauty pageant? Listen as some women talk about what their friend(s) in the pageant did last night, and as others talk about what they are doing today to calm themselves before the final competition begins. As you listen to each contestant, decide whether she is talking about last night or today. You will hear each set of statements twice.

	1	2	3	4	5	6	7	8
Anoche								
Hoy								

Actividad 8

Even though pets cannot express their emotions through words, they can express themselves through their actions. As you hear each person describe his or her pet's behavior, match a picture to the pet. Write the number of each pet owner's description underneath the picture of his or her dog. You will hear each description twice.

____

____

____

____

____

____

Realidades 2

Capítulo 6A

Nombre ______________________ Hora ________

Fecha ______________________

AUDIO

Actividad 9

Yesterday in her popular talk show "**Dime la verdad,**" Lola Lozano had as her guests a group of famous soccer players. The question on the program was "**¿Qué lo vuelve más loco?**" In the table below, take notes about what each one said. Then, use your notes to complete the sentences about each guest. You will hear each conversation twice.

MIS NOTAS
1.
2.
3.
4.
5.

1. Luis se vuelve loco cuando ______________________.
2. Marisol se vuelve loca cuando ______________________.
3. Enrique se vuelve loco cuando ______________________.
4. María se vuelve loca cuando ______________________ ______________________.
5. Martín se vuelve loco cuando ______________________.

Actividad 10

You and your friend are flipping through the channels, and you have each found one thing that you'd like to watch. Using the pictures below, describe each show in detail. The first description has been started for you.

1.

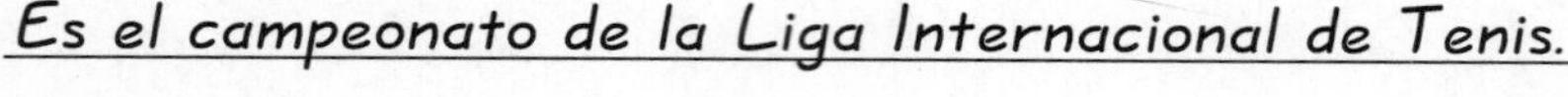
Es el campeonato de la Liga Internacional de Tenis.

____

____

____

____

____

2.

____

____

____

____

____

Nombre _______________ Hora _______________

Fecha _______________

WRITING

Actividad 11

Your Spanish teacher was absent yesterday, and has asked everyone in the class to tell about one thing that happened while he was out. Complete the students' sentences by conjugating the verbs provided in the preterite tense and adding a logical conclusion. Follow the model.

Modelo nosotros / competir

Nosotros competimos en un concurso de belleza para practicar las palabras para describir la ropa.

1. yo / servir

 ____

2. Elena / sentirse

 ____

3. todos nosotros / repetir

 ____

4. Jacques / dormir

 ____

5. tú / reírse

 ____

6. Lola y Raquel / pedir

 ____

7. Pancho y él / sonreír

 ____

8. Susana / mentir

 ____

9. yo / seguir

 ____

10. nosotros / divertirse

 ____

Nombre ______ Hora ______

Fecha ______

WRITING

Actividad 12

Look at the scene below from Mariela and Pablo's wedding. Write at least six sentences to tell what is happening at the moment. You may want to use the verbs **casarse, enojarse, ponerse, aburrirse, dormirse,** and **divertirse.**

Realidades 2 | Nombre | Hora

Capítulo 6A | Fecha | **WRITING**

Actividad 13

Juanita just participated in a beauty pageant, and is writing a letter to her grandmother to tell her what it was like.

A. First, write sentences to help her describe where the event took place, who was there, and what everyone looked like. The first one is done for you.

Estuve en el Teatro Central.

B. Next, list what Juanita and the other contestants probably did during the competition. The first one is done for you.

Yo me vestí en una hora.

C. Finally, use your sentences from Part A and Part B to help Juanita write her letter to her grandmother. The letter has been started for you.

Querida abuela:

Hoy yo participé en un concurso de belleza. ¡Fue fantástico!

VIDEO

Antes de ver el video

Actividad 1

The next video is about a short movie that Manolo directs. Think about movies you have seen recently and answer the following questions using words from your vocabulary.

1. ¿Qué clase de película fue? ______
2. ¿Quiénes eran los actores principales? ______
3. ¿Quién era el (la) director(a)? ______
4. ¿De qué trataba? ______
5. ¿Había mucha violencia o era más un cuento de enamorados? ______

¿Comprendes?

Actividad 2

Answer the following questions in complete sentences in order to better understand the video.

1. ¿Qué está haciendo Ramón en su habitación?

______

2. ¿Quién entra a la habitación cuando Ramón está estudiando?

______

3. ¿Qué quiere hacer Ramón con el periódico?

___

___

4. ¿En qué idiomas puede hablar el mosquito?

___

___

5. ¿Por qué Ramón no mata el mosquito?

___

___

6. ¿Dónde se va a esconder el mosquito el día del examen para explicarle todo a Ramón?

___

___

7. ¿Quién mata el mosquito y cómo lo hace?

___

___

Actividad 3

In the chart below are quotes from the video. Next to each quote, write the name of the character who said it and the role he or she played in the movie. Follow the model.

	Frase u oración	Personaje	Papel
Modelo	"¡¡¡NOOOOOOOO!!!"	*Claudia*	*mosquito*
1.	"Tengo que estudiar y tú me molestas."		
2.	"¡Yo quiero hacer el personaje principal!"		
3.	"¡Ramón, despiértate ya!"		
4.	"A ver... necesito tres actores."		
5.	"¡No, no me mates, por favor!"		
6.	"¿Podemos tener efectos especiales?"		
7.	"Parece que estudiaste mucho."		
8.	"Pero, Teresa, ¿qué has hecho?"		

Y, ¿qué más?

Actividad 4

Now that you have seen the movie made by the characters from the video, think about a film that you might like to create. In the spaces below, list the characters and describe the plot and the scene to get you started.

Los personajes: ______________________________

El argumento: ______________________________

La escena: ______________________________

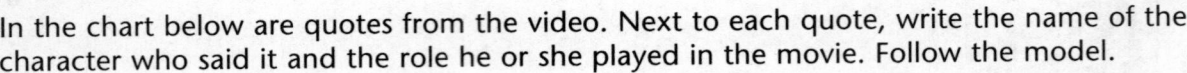

Realidades 2 Nombre Hora

Capítulo 6B Fecha **AUDIO**

Actividad 5

The drama class is trying to decide on the cast of their upcoming spring production **"Aquella noche."** Match the name of the person with his or her suggested role by marking an X in the corresponding square in the grid. You will hear each set of statements twice.

	El (la) ladrón (ladrona)	El galán	El (la) extra-terrestre	El (la) detective	El (la) director(a)	La víctima
Fernando						
María						
Matilde						
Antonio						
Alberto						
Carmen						

Actividad 6

Listen as people talk about movies they have seen. As you hear each opinion, fill in the grid below by writing or circling the correct answer. You do not need to write complete sentences. You will hear each set of statements twice.

	¿La recomienda?	¿El argumento?	¿Qué cosa(s) le gustó/gustaron más?
1.	Sí / No	Básico / Complicado	
2.	Sí / No	Básico / Complicado	
3.	Sí / No	Básico / Complicado	
4.	Sí / No	Básico / Complicado	
5.	Sí / No	Básico / Complicado	

Realidades 2 Nombre ______ Hora ______

Capítulo 6B Fecha ______ **AUDIO**

Actividad 7

In today's episode of **"Dime la verdad,"** Lola Lana interviews actors and actresses on the set of a popular **telenovela.** She quickly learns that they all have very different movie preferences. As you listen, write the number of the interview underneath the corresponding poster. You will hear each set of statements twice.

______

______

______

______

______

Actividad 8

Even though Julia's grandmother only missed one episode of her favorite **telenovela,** she is eager to hear about what she missed. As Julia tells her about the last episode, answer the questions below about what has happened with each character. You will hear each conversation twice.

¿Qué ha pasado?

1. Javier ______
2. Marlena ______
3. Marco ______
4. Victoria ______
5. Marisol ______

Realidades 2 | Nombre ______ | Hora ______

Capítulo 6B | Fecha ______ | AUDIO

Actividad 9

You and your classmates are creating storyboards to outline the plots of your upcoming class movies. Listen as one student describes the plot line for his project. Take notes on each part of the plot in the top half of each of the storyboard boxes below. Then, draw a quick sketch in the bottom half of each box. You will hear the story twice.

NOTES and SKETCHES			
#1	#2	#3	#4
#5	#6	#7	#8

Nombre ______ Hora ______

Fecha ______ **WRITING**

Actividad 10

Look at the movie theater marquee below. For each movie, write at least three sentences to tell what you think it might be about. The first one has been started for you.

1. *"Un verano que recordar" es una película romántica.*

______

2. ______

3. ______

Actividad 11

A. You are interested in hosting an exchange student from Spain. Fill out the form below so that your school can find you a compatible student.

Nombre ______
Edad *(age)* ______
Actividad(es) que te gusta(n) ______
Comida(s) que te encanta(n) ______
Clase(s) que te interesa(n) ______
Tipo(s) de película(s) que te fascina(n) ______
Cosa(s) que te disgusta(n) ______

B. Now, read Ramiro's form below and write complete sentences to compare your interests with his. Follow the model.

Nombre *Ramiro Fuentes*
Edad *16*
Actividad(es) que te gusta(n) *esquiar, leer, ir al cine*
Comida(s) que te encanta(n) *la carne, la pasta, los pasteles*
Clase(s) que te interesa(n) *ciencias naturales, inglés*
Tipo(s) de película(s) que te fascina(n) *románticas, de horror*
Cosa(s) que te disgusta(n) *la televisión, los gatos*

Modelo *A Ramiro le gusta leer pero a mí me disgusta. Prefiero más escribir.*

1. ______
2. ______
3. ______
4. ______
5. ______

C. Based on your interests, do you think you and Ramiro are compatible? Why or why not? Write your answer in Spanish in one or two complete sentences.

______
______
______

Actividad 12

Before becoming a host family to a Mexican exchange student, your family is asked to provide a list of things you have done to become familiar with Mexican culture. Under each category below, write three sentences about your real or imaginary experiences. The first one has been done for you.

Los viajes

Nosotros *hemos viajado a Cancún y hemos visitado las ruinas mayas.*

Yo _______________

Mi hermano _______________

Los deportes

Mi familia y yo _______________

Mi clase de español _______________

Mis padres _______________

Las clases

Yo _______________

Mi hermano(a) _______________

Mis hermanos(as) _______________

Las comidas

Mi madre _______________

Yo _______________

Toda la familia _______________

Actividad 13

You are writing a review for the school newspaper of a movie that you saw recently.

A. First, write down the information requested below to give some background information about the movie. You may use your imagination.

1. Nombre del actor principal ______________________

   Otras películas de él ______________________

2. Nombre de la actriz principal ______________________

   Otras películas de ella ______________________

3. Nombre del director (de la directora) ______________________

   Otras películas de él (ella) ______________________

B. Now, write five sentences about your opinion of the movie. Tell what you liked, what you disliked, what interested you, etc. about the plot, acting, and directing of the movie.

____
____
____
____
____

C. Now, write your review for the paper, using the information from Part A and Part B to help you.

____
____
____
____
____
____
____
____

Realidades 2 Nombre _______________ Hora _______

Capítulo 7A Fecha _______________ VIDEO

Antes de ver el video

Actividad 1

List eight ingredients that you would need to prepare your favorite dish.

_______________ _______________

_______________ _______________

_______________ _______________

_______________ _______________

¿Comprendes?

Actividad 2

Javier is teaching Ignacio how to make paella. The steps he takes and the things he tells Ignacio are listed below, but they are in the wrong order. Order them correctly by writing a **1** to indicate the first thing Javier said and a **7** to indicate the last thing he said.

a. ______ ¡No tires el aceite! Y no añadas más. Ya tienes más que suficiente.

b. ______ No uso ingredientes congelados. Sólo uso ingredientes frescos... por eso mi paella es tan rica.

c. ______ Bueno, está bien. Pero primero vamos al supermercado..., a comprar los ingredientes.

d. ______ Primero tienes que calentar el aceite, en una sartén grande; como ésta.

e. ______ No te olvides del aceite, y no dejes que se caliente demasiado.

f. ______ Quieres decir, vamos a volver a empezar otra vez...

g. ______ Quiero preparar una comida especial para Ana, para su cumpleaños.

Nombre ______________________ Hora ________

Fecha ______________________ **VIDEO**

Actividad 3

You have just finished watching Javier and Ignacio have a cooking adventure. Answer the questions below in complete sentences. Follow the model.

Modelo ¿Adónde van Javier e Ignacio?

Ignacio y Javier van al supermercado a comprar los ingredientes para hacer una paella.

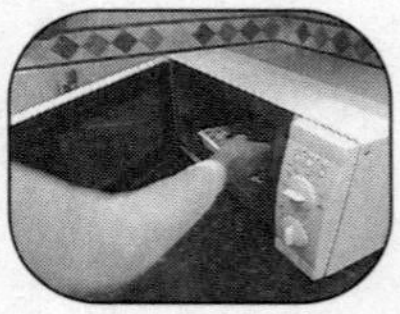

1. ¿Qué sabe cocinar Ignacio?

____

____

2. ¿Cómo es la paella de Javier? ¿Por qué?

____

____

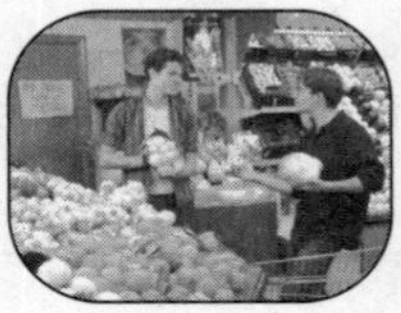

3. ¿Qué van a necesitar los jóvenes para hacer la paella?

____

____

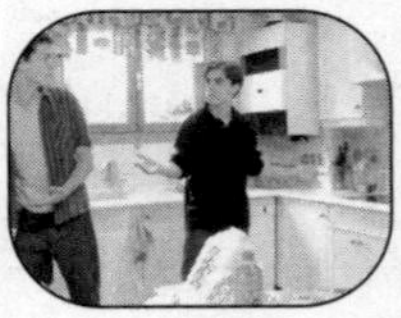

4. ¿Dónde se prepara la paella?

____

____

5. ¿Qué tiene que hacer Ignacio con los ajos antes de cocinarlos?

____

____

6. ¿Por qué piensa Javier que Ana va a recibir una gran sorpresa, que no va a ser buena?

Y, ¿qué más?

Actividad 4

Do you like to have big dinner parties or intimate dinners for two? What would you prepare for such a dinner? Write a short paragraph to tell about your ideal gathering and its menu. Follow the model.

Modelo *A mí me gusta reunirme con mis mejores amigos.*

En estas reuniones, me gusta cocinar algo como un pescado en salsa de queso. Invito a varios amigos, y ellos traen los otros platos: la ensalada, la bebida y el postre.

Nos ponemos a cocinar todos, y escuchamos música mientras preparamos la cena. Al terminar, todos comemos una comida muy rica, y todos quedamos contentos de compartir una noche tan agradable.

Nombre ______________________ Hora ______

Fecha ______________________

AUDIO

Actividad 5

Alejandro's older sister has been trying to teach him the basics of cooking. Listen to the questions he asks her during one of their phone conversations. If the question seems logical, circle the word **lógico** and if the question seems illogical, circle the word **ilógico.** You will hear each question twice.

1.	**lógico**	**ilógico**	**5.**	**lógico**	**ilógico**
2.	**lógico**	**ilógico**	**6.**	**lógico**	**ilógico**
3.	**lógico**	**ilógico**	**7.**	**lógico**	**ilógico**
4.	**lógico**	**ilógico**	**8.**	**lógico**	**ilógico**

Actividad 6

Both Ignacio and Javier think they are expert cooks. As they are preparing paella, each wants to make sure the other is doing it right. Listen to their conversations, and match each one to one of the pictures below. Write the number of the conversation in the blank underneath the corresponding picture. You will hear each conversation twice.

______

______

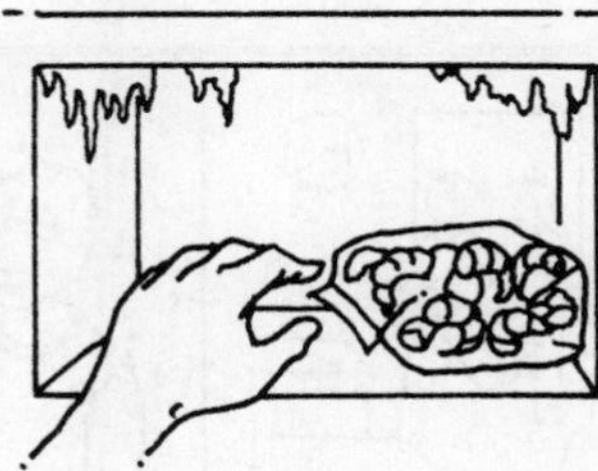

______

______

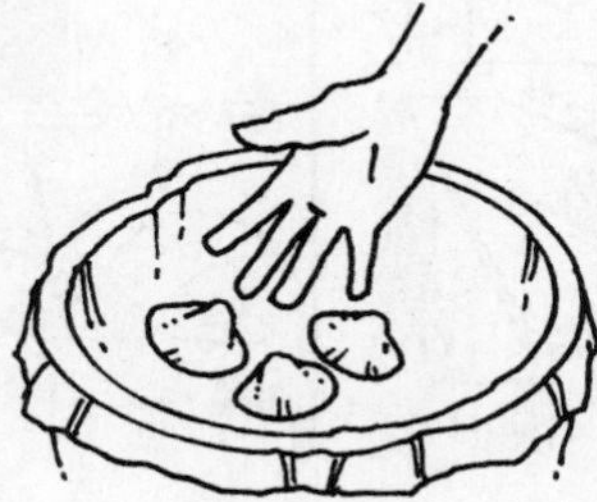

______

______

Actividad 7

Listen as different people give Roberto advice about cooking. As you listen to each piece of advice, decide whether the person is advising him on: a) getting ready to cook; b) things to do while he's cooking; or c) things to do after he's finished cooking. Place an **X** in the appropriate box in the grid below. You will hear each piece of advice twice.

	1	2	3	4	5	6	7	8	9	10
Antes de cocinar...										
Cuando cocinas...										
Después de cocinar...										

Actividad 8

Listen as a counselor at a Spanish Immersion Camp tells the campers what things are going to be like at the camp for the summer. Draw a circle around the things that do happen, and an **X** over the pictures of the things that don't happen. You will hear each statement twice.

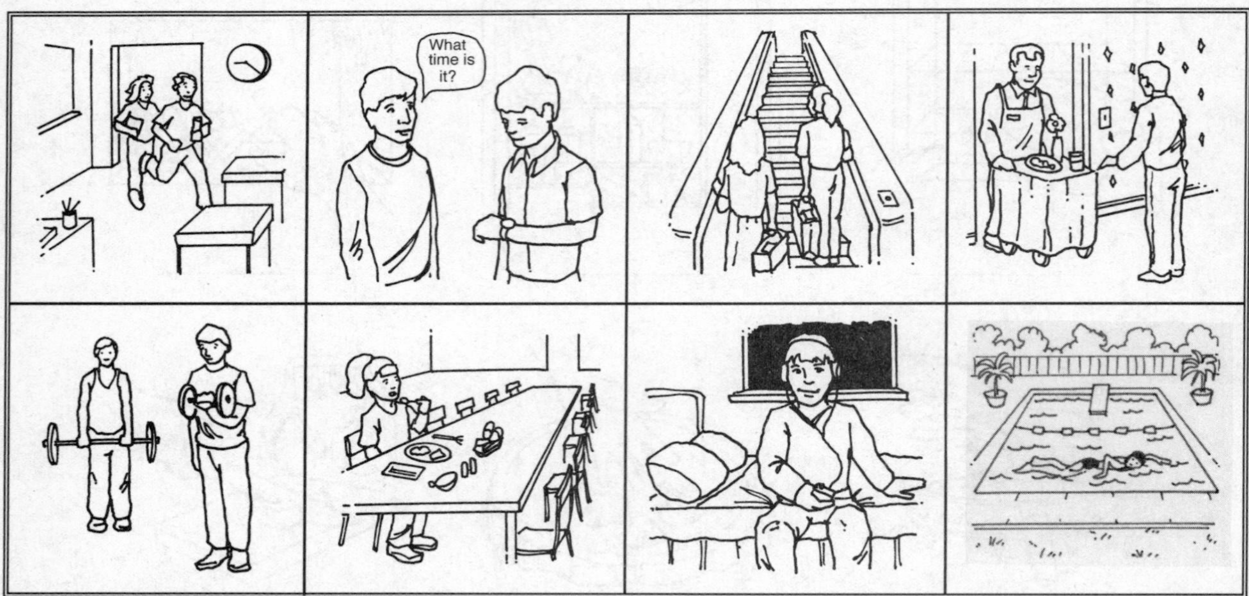

Realidades 2 Nombre _______________ Hora _______

Capítulo 7A Fecha _______________ **AUDIO**

Actividad 9

Ryan's friend, Carmen, asks him to come to dinner at her home. Some of the things he eats are very familiar, but others are not. Listen as they talk about what is on the dinner table. Write the number of each conversation under the corresponding item on the dinner table. You will hear each conversation twice.

Nombre ______ Hora ______

Fecha ______ **WRITING**

Actividad 10

Your mother is running late and calls you from the store to tell you to get dinner started. Use the pictures below to write what she tells you to do. Follow the model.

Modelo *Fríe el pollo en una sartén*.

1. ______.

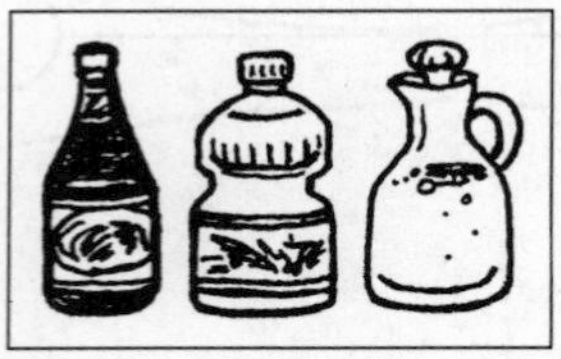

2. ______.

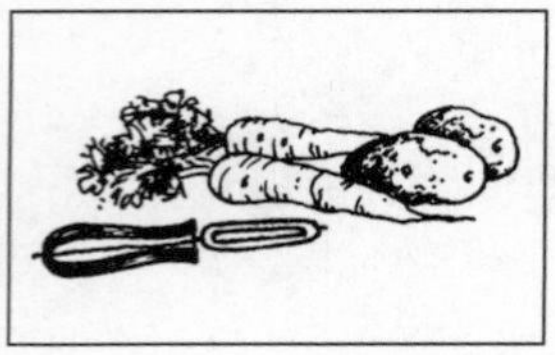

3. ______.

4. ______.

5. ______.

6. ______.

Actividad 11

Pancho is sick and goes to the doctor, who tells him what *not* to do if he wants to get better quickly. Write the doctor's instructions using the verbs below and your imagination. Follow the model.

hablar	comer	beber	ir
ser	dormir	empezar	jugar

Modelo *No comas ni las papas fritas ni los pasteles cuando estás enfermo.*

1. ______
2. ______
3. ______
4. ______
5. ______
6. ______
7. ______
8. ______

Actividad 12

A Spanish-speaking friend wants you to mail her your recipe for gazpacho. You are looking at the recipe card in your files, but decide it would be better to write out the instructions in addition to the information on the file. Write out instructions for how to prepare the gazpacho, as shown in the first item.

Receta para el gazpacho

Se necesitan:

Modo de preparación:

1. cortar
2. poner en una licuadora (*blender*)
3. picar
4. añadir
5. mezclar
6. probar
7. añadir
8. servir

1. *Se cortan el pepino (cucumber) y los tomates* .
2. ____.
3. ____.
4. ____.
5. ____.
6. ____.
7. ____.
8. ____.

Actividad 13

A. Your school is opening up a kitchen for students to use. Help the administration set rules for its use by first writing a list of the things that one can and should do there. Follow the model.

Modelo *Se usa el microondas para recalentar la comida* .

1. ________________.
2. ________________.
3. ________________.
4. ________________.
5. ________________.
6. ________________.

B. Now, set limits by writing a list of six things that students should *not* do there. Follow the model.

Modelo *No tires la comida en la cocina* .

1. ________________.
2. ________________.
3. ________________.
4. ________________.
5. ________________.
6. ________________.

Antes de ver el video

Actividad 1

Make a list of six things you would bring to a picnic.

1. ____________ 4. ____________
2. ____________ 5. ____________
3. ____________ 6. ____________

Now, name three activities you might do on a picnic.

1. ____________
2. ____________
3. ____________

Finally, name two things that could happen to spoil your picnic.

1. ____________
2. ____________

¿Comprendes?

Actividad 2

All of the following sentences are incorrect. Rewrite them to make them correct.

1. Manolo es del campo y no le gusta comer en la ciudad.

____

2.  Claudia trae en la canasta toda la comida que preparó.

____

3. Los muchachos van al parque en el coche de Claudia.

____

4. En el parque nadie hace fogatas.

____

5. En el parque no hay puestos de comida; no pueden comprar nada.

____

6. A Manolo le encanta la comida que hace Claudia.

____

Actividad 3

Answer the following questions in complete sentences based on the video.

1. ¿Por qué a Manolo no le gusta comer en el campo?

____

2. ¿Por qué Claudia no puede darles bebidas a los amigos?

____

3. ¿Por qué escogen un sitio para sentarse por fin?

____

4. ¿Quiénes dan una caminata por el parque?

____

5. ¿Qué comida trajo Claudia? ¿Por qué?

____

Y, ¿qué más?

Actividad 4

Picnics are a fun summer activity. Make a list telling what kind of food and beverage you like to bring to a picnic, who you like to invite, and where you like to have it. Use complete sentences. The first one has been done for you.

1. *Me gusta traer una canasta con mucha comida cuando quiero hacer un picnic.*
2. ______
3. ______
4. ______
5. ______
6. ______
7. ______

Actividad 5

The Cruz and Ramos families are getting together for their annual barbecue. Listen as they talk about what they brought in their picnic baskets. As you listen to each family member talk about a particular food item, look at the pictures below of the picnic baskets. Then, write **C** in the blank if you think a member of the Cruz family is speaking, and write **R** in the blank if you think a member of the Ramos family is speaking. You will hear each set of statements twice.

1. ______ 5. ______
2. ______ 6. ______
3. ______ 7. ______
4. ______ 8. ______

Realidades 2 Nombre Hora

Capítulo 7B Fecha **AUDIO**

Actividad 6

Some people prefer the great outdoors and others prefer the comforts of being indoors. As you listen to each conversation, determine whether the person is talking about eating outdoors or inside at a restaurant. Fill in the grid below as you listen. You will hear each set of statements twice.

	1	2	3	4	5	6

Actividad 7

You are helping the Scoutmaster, Sr. Naranjo, assign tasks for the boys in his troop to do at summer camp. Your job is to write each task in the chart below so that each pair of boys knows what to do. You will hear each task twice.

Carlos y Ramón	*Lleven los sacos de dormir.*
1. Dani y Benito	
2. Adán y Miguel	
3. David y Enrique	
4. Jaime y Pepe	
5. Arturo y Benito	
6. Raúl y Tomás	

Actividad 8

Listen as people talk about what they did on behalf of their friends or relatives last week. As you listen to each conversation, fill in the grid below with the following information: 1) what he or she did; 2) on whose behalf he or she did it; and 3) the amount of time it took. For the first column, choose from the following statements: **a) Preparó una cena; b) Trabajó en una computadora; c) Estudió matemáticas; d) Limpió el apartamento.** You will hear each set of statements twice.

	¿Qué hizo?	¿Por quién lo hizo?	¿Por cuánto tiempo lo hizo?
1.			_______ horas
2.			_______ horas
3.			_______ horas
4.			_______ horas

Actividad 9

Listen as guests on a cruise ship listen to instructions from the Activity Director about the upcoming "ship-to-shore" camping trip. She gives lots of advice on what to do on their expedition. As you listen to each piece of advice, decide whether she is talking about trekking in the woods or getting ready for the evening barbecue and bonfire. Put an X in the correct box below. You will hear each piece of advice twice.

	1	2	3	4	5	6	7	8	9	10
Consejos para el caminante										
Consejos para hacer una barbacoa y fogata										

Realidades 2 | Nombre ______ | Hora ______

Capítulo 7B | Fecha ______ | **WRITING**

Actividad 10

Look at the picture below of the picnic Adriana recently had with her family. Help her write a letter to her pen pal describing the picnic. The letter has been started for you.

Querida Laura,

Mi familia y yo decidimos comer al aire libre porque hacía sol ese día.

______

______

______

______

______

______

______

______

Saludos,

Adriana

Realidades 2 Nombre ______ Hora ______

Capítulo 7B Fecha ______ **WRITING**

Actividad 11

Your teachers are making lists of rules for their classrooms. For each class below, write four rules. Write two rules about what the students have to do in the class, and two about what the teacher must do in the class. Follow the model.

1. Tecnología
   los estudiantes
   No traigan ni comida ni bebidas a la clase.
   ______
   el (la) profesor(a)
   Empiece la clase a tiempo.
   ______

2. Arte
   los estudiantes
   ______
   ______
   el (la) profesor(a)
   ______
   ______

3. Educación física
   los estudiantes
   ______
   ______
   el (la) profesor(a)
   ______
   ______

4. Biología
   los estudiantes
   ______
   ______
   el (la) profesor(a)
   ______
   ______

Actividad 12

Answer the following questions in complete sentences that include the word **por,** where applicable.

1. ¿Qué fue la última cosa que compraste? ¿Cuánto pagaste?

2. Por lo general, ¿gastas mucho cuando vas de compras? ¿Por qué?

3. Cuando quieres mandar una tarjeta a un amigo, ¿cómo la mandas?

4. ¿Cómo te comunicas con tus amigos durante un viaje?

5. ¿Cómo viaja tu familia si quiere ir de vacaciones?

6. ¿Cuándo fue la última vez que viajaste con tu familia? ¿Por cuánto tiempo estuvieron de vacaciones?

7. ¿Uds. caminaron mucho allí? Si no, ¿cómo pasaron de un lugar a otro?

8. ¿Cómo es un día normal para ti? ¿En qué es diferente un día de vacaciones?

Realidades 2 | Nombre | Hora

Capítulo 7B | Fecha | **WRITING**

Actividad 13

Your entire Spanish class is coming to your house for a barbecue next weekend. They have asked you to e-mail them and let them know what to bring. Write three complete sentences for each group. Follow the model.

Modelo Celia y Ramón: *Vengan a mi casa a las once. Traigan la mayonesa, la mostaza y la salsa de tomate. No se olviden del cuchillo para servirlos.*

1. La Srta. Arrojo: ______________________________

2. Catrina, Ramona y Carlos: ______________________________

3. Luisa y David: ______________________________

B. Luisa and David would also like to bring a fruit salad, and have asked you to send them the directions from a cookbook for making one. Write at least six instructions you would find in the recipe for making a fruit salad. The first one has been done for you.

Compren las uvas, las manzanas, los plátanos y la piña en el supermercado.

Realidades 2 Nombre Hora

Capítulo 8A Fecha **VIDEO**

Antes de ver el video

Actividad 1

There are many ways to travel: by plane, boat, bus, train, or car. Mark with an **X** the method of transportation you think would be best for each situation.

situaciones	avión	barco	autobús	coche	tren
Tengo sólo una semana de vacaciones y está lejos.					
Estamos planeando ir a Aruba, la isla en el mar Caribe.					
Somos estudiantes y no tenemos mucho dinero.					
Sólo puedo ir al acto de graduación por el fin de semana.					
No me gusta manejar, pero me encanta ver el paisaje.					
Quiero llegar rápido para estar más tiempo con mis primos.					
No está tan lejos, somos muchos y tenemos mucho equipaje.					
Lo más divertido es conocer todas las islas.					
Está lejos pero hay varios pueblos interesantes por el camino.					

Realidades 2 | Nombre ______ | Hora ______

Capítulo 8A | Fecha ______ | VIDEO

¿Comprendes?

Actividad 2

Ana is writing to a friend about her upcoming trip. Some of her statements are true and some are false. If the statement is true, write **cierto.** If the statement is false, rewrite it to make it true.

1. Elena y yo estamos planeando un viaje a Rusia para estudiar ruso.
______
2. Esta mañana fuimos a la agencia de viajes para comprar el billete.
______
3. Un vuelo directo a Londres en avión cuesta cincuenta euros ida y vuelta.
______
4. Decidimos viajar en tren y viajamos en el "eurostar" para ir de Barcelona a Londres.
______
5. Compramos el billete para estudiantes. La agente nos dijo que muchos niños viajan así.
______
6. El viaje dura como catorce horas y quince minutos.
______
7. Ya hicimos la reserva.
______

Actividad 3

Answer the following questions based on what happened in the video.

1. ¿Por qué está Ana tan impaciente en la agencia de viajes?
______
2. ¿Para qué van Ana y Elena a Londres y por cuánto tiempo?
______

3. ¿Cómo quieren ir a Londres? ______

4. ¿Qué sugerencia les hace la agente de viajes? ______

______

5. ¿Qué tipo más barato de billete pueden comprar? ______

6. ¿Por qué Elena no está muy segura de viajar en tren?

______

7. ¿Cómo deciden finalmente viajar a Londres las muchachas?

______

8. ¿Por qué Elena y Ana tienen que regresar a la agencia?

______

Y, ¿qué más?

Actividad 4

Think about a trip you would like to take one day with a friend or family member. Answer the following questions to help create your itinerary.

¿Qué sitio te gustaría conocer en estas vacaciones?

______

¿Cómo quieres viajar?

______

¿Con quién te gustaría ir?

______

¿Cuánto tiempo tienes para hacer el viaje?

______

¿Qué documentos necesitas para el viaje?

______

Actividad 5

Listen to the messages recorded by different airlines for customers to listen to as they wait for the next available agent to take their phone call. As you listen to each announcement, identify which picture best matches each taped message. Write the number of the conversation in the blank under the corresponding picture. You will hear each message twice.

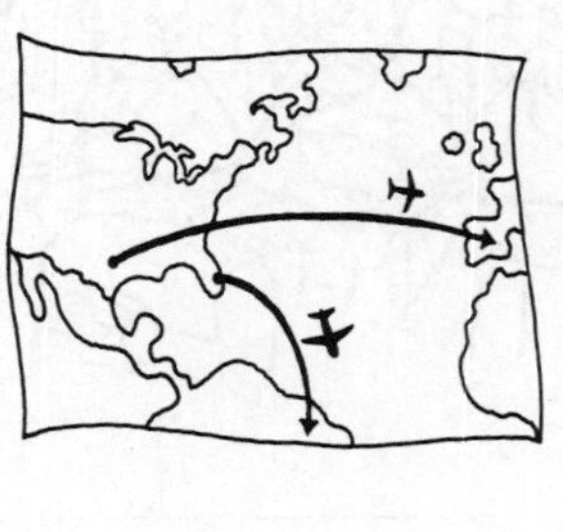
______

______

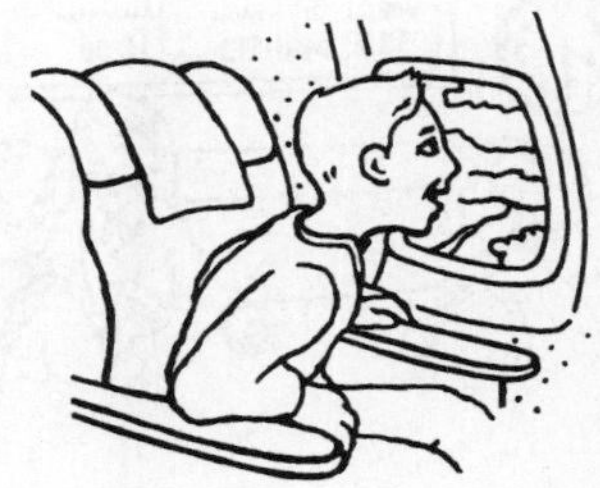
______

______

______

______

Actividad 6

Several Spanish club members just got back from a summer trip to Europe with their teacher. On the way home from the airport, two girls talk about what happened on the trip and how their classmates acted. As you listen, decide whether the student they are talking about was a **buen(a) turista** or **mal(a) turista** and mark the grid below with your answer. You will hear each conversation twice.

	1	2	3	4	5	6
Buen(a) turista						
Mal(a) turista						

AUDIO

Actividad 7

When her friends and family find out that Elisa is going on a school trip to Europe, they all have advice for her about her initial plane trip to Madrid. As you listen to each person's advice, match his or her suggestion to the corresponding picture below. Write the number of the conversation underneath the correct drawing. You will hear each suggestion twice.

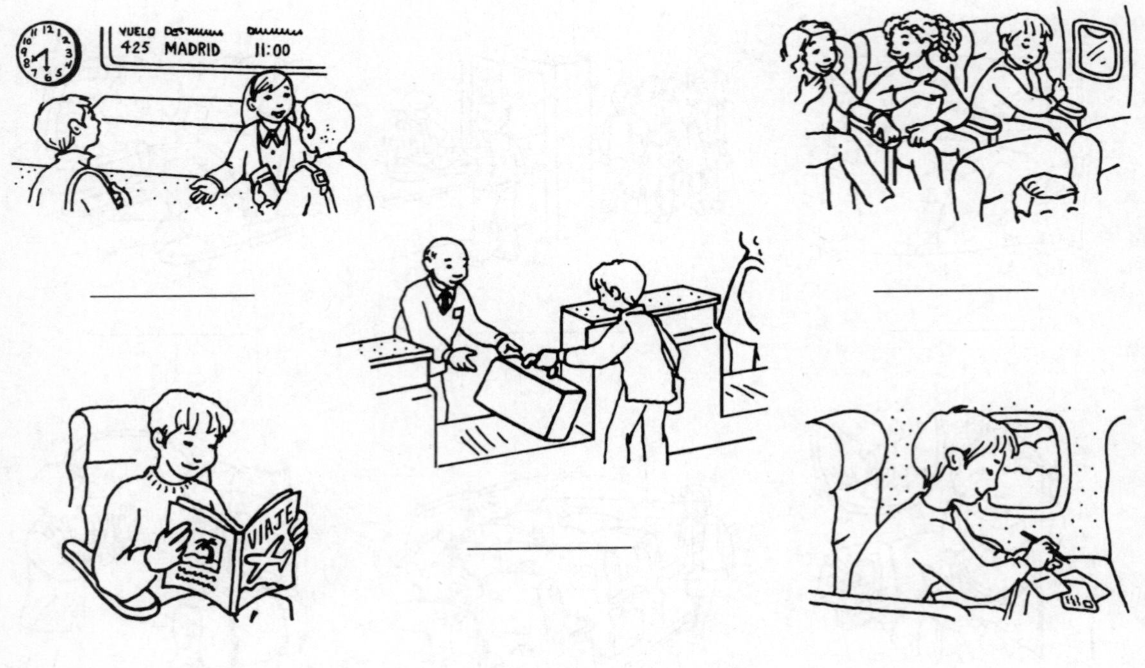

Actividad 8

Listen to a panel of seasoned travelers and school officials as they give suggestions to students who are taking a trip next month. As you listen to each suggestion, decide whether it is a: **a) sugerencia para planear el viaje; b) sugerencia para el aeropuerto y durante el vuelo; c) sugerencia para cuando viajan por las ciudades que visitan;** or **d) sugerencia sobre qué comprar como recuerdo del viaje.** Write the correct letter in each space below. You will hear each suggestion twice.

1. ______ **3.** ______ **5.** ______ **7.** ______ **9.** ______

2. ______ **4.** ______ **6.** ______ **8.** ______ **10.** ______

Nombre ______ Hora ______

Fecha ______ AUDIO

Actividad 9

People sometimes encounter difficulties while traveling. As you listen to each of these three people discuss his or her problem, determine what the problem is and circle the appropriate answer. You will hear each discussion twice.

Viajero(a)	Problema
Sr. Machado	**a.** Necesita ir a Chile para una reunión importante por la tarde. **b.** No tiene su pasaporte para pasar por la aduana. **c.** Su vuelo directo a Buenos Aires llega demasiado tarde.
Sra. Manizales	**a.** Perdió a su mejor amigo en el aeropuerto. **b.** Olvidó el oso de peluche de su hija en el avión. **c.** Olvidó una maleta en el avión.
Luis	**a.** Él es muy impaciente. **b.** Tiene miedo de las inspecciones de seguridad. **c.** Llegó tarde al avión.

Actividad 10

You are showing your friend Ricardo your pictures from a recent trip to Guatemala. Because Ricardo has never traveled by plane, he is curious about what it was like. Describe your trip to him, using the photos below to help you.

1 ______________________________.

2. ______________________________.

3. ______________________________.

4. ______________________________.

5. ______________________________.

6. ______________________________.

7. ______________________________.

8. ______________________________.

Actividad 11

Two new students at your school are asking you how to succeed in Spanish class. Answer their questions below in complete sentences.

BERTO: Nos gustaría saber más de la clase de español. Por ejemplo, ¿cuántas horas recomiendas que nosotros estudiemos todas las noches?

TÚ: ______________________________

____

TITO: ¿Sugieres que nosotros tomemos la clase del profesor Álvarez?

TÚ: ______________________________

____

BERTO: ¿El profesor Álvarez permite que los estudiantes usen los libros en los exámenes?

TÚ: ______________________________

____

TITO: ¿Qué más prefiere él que los estudiantes hagan?

TÚ: ______________________________

____

BERTO: ¿Qué prohíbe que su clase haga?

TÚ: ______________________________

____

TITO: Otra pregunta: ¿La escuela insiste en que yo tome tres años de español?

TÚ: ______________________________

____

BERTO: Muchas gracias por tu ayuda. ¿Tienes más recomendaciones para nosotros?

TÚ: ______________________________

____

____

Realidades 2 Nombre ____ Hora ____

Capítulo 8A Fecha ____ **WRITING**

Actividad 12

A. Some students and teachers are having an informal discussion in the cafeteria about some issues at school. Combine a subject and verb from **Columna A** with a logical subject and verb from **Columna B** to write complete sentences telling what some of the issues are. You may need to add some information to complete the sentences. Follow the model.

Columna A	Columna B
Nosotros/querer	yo/saber el vocabulario
Los profesores/preferir	tú/ser malo
El principal/prohibir	los profesores/no dar exámenes
La profesora de francés/insistir en	nosotros/ir a clase
Yo/recomendar	tú/estar despierto

Modelo *Nosotros queremos que los profesores no den exámenes los lunes.*

1. ____
2. ____
3. ____
4. ____

B. Now, write three recommendations to your own school's administration using the verbs **ser, estar, ir, saber,** or **dar**.

1. ____
2. ____
3. ____

Actividad 13

Your friend Rosario is coming to visit you from Ecuador next week. She is a bit nervous about traveling by plane alone, so you write her an e-mail reminding her of what to do while traveling. Complete the e-mail below with advice for Rosario.

Fecha: 9/4/12
Sujeto: Algunas recomendaciones
Recipiente: rosario@xyz.xyz
De: ____________________
Mensaje: Hola, Rosario. No puedo esperar hasta tu llegada. Antes de ir al aeropuerto, quiero que des el número de tu vuelo a tus padres.

____

____

____

____

____

____

____

____

____

____

____

____

____

¡Buena suerte y te veo pronto!

____

Realidades 2 | Nombre ______ | Hora ______

Capítulo 8B | Fecha ______ | VIDEO

Antes de ver el video

Actividad 1

What are the first things you want to do when you arrive in a new city? Make a list of five activities you would do upon arriving in a foreign city. Follow the model.

Modelo *Caminar*

1. ______
2. ______
3. ______
4. ______
5. ______

¿Comprendes?

Actividad 2

Read each of the following descriptions and decide whether it describes Ignacio, Javier, or both (**los dos**). Circle the correct answer for each.

1.	Tiene un partido de fútbol mañana.	**Ignacio**	**Javier**	**Los dos**
2.	Quiere comprar alguna artesanía.	**Ignacio**	**Javier**	**Los dos**
3.	Compra una guía.	**Ignacio**	**Javier**	**Los dos**
4.	Es la primera vez que visita Toledo sin sus padres.	**Ignacio**	**Javier**	**Los dos**
5.	Quiere regatear por la espada (*sword*).	**Ignacio**	**Javier**	**Los dos**
6.	Le gusta la ciudad de Toledo.	**Ignacio**	**Javier**	**Los dos**
7.	Compra unas tarjetas postales.	**Ignacio**	**Javier**	**Los dos**
8.	Dice que está cansado.	**Ignacio**	**Javier**	**Los dos**

Nombre ______________________ Hora ______

Fecha ______________________

VIDEO

Actividad 3

Next to each video scene, write a sentence describing what was happening at that moment in the video. Follow the model.

Ignacio y Javier van a dejar sus cosas en el hotel.

1. ____

2. ____

3. ____

4. ____

5. ____

6. ____

7. ____

Realidades 2 | Nombre ______ | Hora ______

Capítulo 8B | Fecha ______ | VIDEO

Y, ¿qué más?

Actividad 4

Your friend is going on her first plane trip out of the country. Write five sentences of advice for her. Follow the model.

Modelo *Te aconsejo que tengas siempre buenos modales con la gente.*

Realidades 2 Nombre Hora

Capítulo 8B Fecha **AUDIO**

Actividad 5

Listen as several tourists in Spain call the front desk of the hotel for assistance. Then, write the number of the phone call under the corresponding picture. You will hear each phone call twice.

______

______

______

______

Actividad 6

A student tour group is on the train to begin a two-day tour of the historic town of Toledo, Spain. Eager to use the Spanish they have learned, they talk to some of the Spanish-speaking passengers on the train. As you listen to each conversation, place a check mark under the picture of the place they are talking about in the grid below. You will hear each conversation twice.

1				
2				
3				
4				
5				

Actividad 7

Although Sra. Milano wants her Spanish students to enjoy their first trip to Spain, she also wants to be sure that they behave appropriately while they are there. Listen as she gives them advice at their last meeting before they leave on their trip. Categorize her advice as suggestions for how to: a) act in the hotel; b) dress while touring; c) stay safe on the trip; and d) interact with the people who live there. Mark with an X the appropriate box as you listen to each recommendation. You will hear each recommendation twice.

	1	2	3	4	5	6	7
Hotel behavior							
Appropriate dress							
Safety							
Interacting with people							

Realidades 2 | Nombre ______ | Hora ______

Capítulo 8B | Fecha ______ | **AUDIO**

Actividad 8

A few graduating seniors have recorded messages with advice for the underclassmen in their schools. Match each senior with the topics of his or her advice by placing a check mark in the corresponding box. You will hear each message twice.

	pedir ayuda	sentirse contento	reírse	recordar a los amigos	no perder tiempo (*waste time*)	divertirse	no mentir	seguir sus sueños
Isabel								
Jorge								
Lisa								
Beto								

Actividad 9

Listen as teenagers use their international calling cards to talk to their parents while they travel in Spain. Based on what each says, match a picture below to the main idea of his or her conversation. You will hear each conversation twice.

______

______

______

______

______

Realidades 2 Nombre Hora

Capítulo 8B Fecha **WRITING**

Actividad 10

You are working at a travel agency answering e-mails from travelers who have questions. Read their questions below and answer them in complete sentences.

1. Mi esposo y yo queremos hacer una reservación en un hotel. ¿Qué tipo de habitación debemos conseguir?

2. ¿Cómo es un buen turista? ¿Qué cosa no hace?

3. ¿Qué actividades puedo hacer en el lago Ontario?

4. Voy a Madrid y no sé qué lugares debo visitar. ¿Dónde busco esta información?

5. En los mercados de México, ¿debemos aceptar el precio que el vendedor nos dice?

6. ¿A quiénes les doy una propina en los Estados Unidos?

7. Cuando llego al hotel, ¿adónde voy?

8. ¿Adónde voy para cambiar dinero al llegar a Argentina?

Realidades 2 | Nombre ______ | Hora ______

Capítulo 8B | Fecha ______ | WRITING

Actividad 11

Your school has handed out a survey to students in order find out their opinions on different topics related to school life. Write two opinions for each category below, using complete sentences. The first one has been done for you.

1. la comida

   Es importante que sirvan pizza todos los días.

   Quiero que preparen galletas de chocolate.

2. los autobuses

   ______

   ______

3. las horas de la escuela

   ______

   ______

4. las clases

   ______

   ______

5. los deportes

   ______

   ______

6. los profesores

   ______

   ______

7. los estudiantes

   ______

   ______

Realidades 2 Nombre ____________________ Hora ________

Capítulo 8B Fecha ____________________ **WRITING**

Actividad 12

You are helping your Health teacher make fliers for Health Awareness Week. Using the phrases below, write six recommendations on the flier to the people indicated in the parentheses. Then, write six recommendations about what they should avoid. Use complete sentences. The first one has been done for you.

jugar a los deportes (los jóvenes)

perder peso (los estadounidenses)

acostarse temprano (tú)

comenzar un programa de ejercicio (los estudiantes)

seguir las sugerencias del médico (nosotros)

pedir comida saludable (la gente)

~~dormir ocho horas (nosotros)~~

LA SEMANA DE LA SALUD

- *Nos recomienda que durmamos ocho horas cada noche.*

  Es mejor que no comamos muchas galletas.
- ____________________

  ____
- ____________________

  ____
- ____________________

  ____
- ____________________

  ____
- ____________________

  ____

Realidades 2 | Nombre | Hora

Capítulo 8B | Fecha | **WRITING**

Actividad 13

Your younger brother and sister are going on a trip to Spain with their class and have asked you to help them get ready.

A. First, organize your thoughts by writing appropriate responses to their questions below.

¿Qué debemos traer al aeropuerto?

¿Qué/A quiénes vamos a encontrar en el aeropuerto?

B. Now, give your siblings advice about their trip using the ideas you wrote above. Follow the model.

Modelo A tu hermano:

Es necesario que traigas tu carnet de identificación al aeropuerto.

A tu hermana:

A los dos:

Realidades 2 Nombre ______ Hora ______

Capítulo 9A Fecha ______ **VIDEO**

Antes de ver el video

Actividad 1

There are many different professions and careers you might choose to pursue. In the first column below, write five professions or careers that interest you. In the second column, write something with which each career or profession is associated. The first one is done for you.

Carrera o profesión	Cosas
Profesor(a)	*la educación*

¿Comprendes?

Actividad 2

Each of the following sentences is false. Rewrite each one to make it true.

1. Angélica prefiere el mundo de las artes.

______

2. Pedro dijo: "A mí me gusta todo tipo de arte. Y me encanta correr."

______

3. Pedro podría ser médico; le gusta mucho escribir.

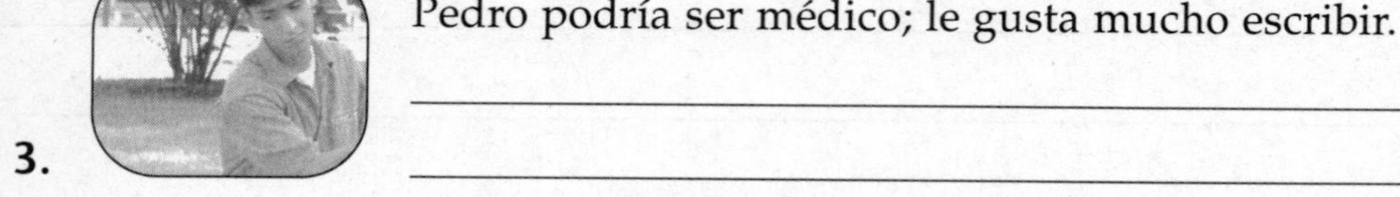

______

4. Esteban quiere estudiar para ingeniero o contador. Le gustan las profesiones técnicas.

____

5. Esteban pide la dirección electrónica de Pedro.

____

Actividad 3

Answer each of the following questions in complete sentences based on what you saw in the video.

1. ¿Por qué quieren ir los amigos al colegio un domingo?

____

2. ¿Qué dice Angélica cuando ve el dibujo de Pedro?

____

3. ¿Cómo prefiere Angélica ganarse la vida algún día?

____

4. ¿Cómo prefiere Esteban ganarse la vida algún día?

____

5. ¿Cuándo van a graduarse los amigos?

____

6. ¿Por qué dice Pedro: "Gracias, es un momento muy importante para mí"?

____

Y, ¿qué más?

Actividad 4

The friends from the video seem to know what they want to be when they are older. Think about the five professions you wrote about in **Actividad 1** and how you can work towards achieving each goal. Use the model to guide you.

Modelo *Para ser profesora yo necesito ir a la universidad y estudiar educación. También necesito aprender a enseñar la clase.*

1. ______________________________

2. ______________________________

3. ______________________________

4. ______________________________

5. ______________________________

Realidades  Nombre ______ Hora ______

Capítulo 9A Fecha ______ **AUDIO**

Actividad 5

Listen to the following students describe their interests and talents, then match each one up with his or her ideal career by writing the number of the statement under the corresponding picture. You will hear each statement twice.

______

______

______

______

______

______

Actividad 6

Listen to the latest listings that were recently posted on a job hotline. Match the job qualifications with each of the pictures below by writing the number of each conversation underneath the corresponding picture. You will hear each listing twice.

Actividad 7

Listen as friends get together and talk about what they would like to do as a career in the future. What seems to motivate each of them the most? Is it: a) the imagined salary; b) the possibility of fame; or c) the possible benefit of his or her work to society? Listen to each person and place an X in the corresponding box in the grid. You will hear each conversation twice.

	1	2	3	4	5	6	7
¿El salario?							
¿La fama?							
¿Los beneficios a la sociedad?							

Realidades 2 | Nombre ______ | Hora ______

Capítulo 9A | Fecha ______ | AUDIO

Actividad 8

The first day on the job can be a challenge for anyone. Listen as these people are shown around their new offices. As you listen to each conversation, determine what kind of job each person has. In the blanks provided, write the letter of the picture that corresponds to each conversation. You will hear each conversation twice.

A B C D E F

1. ______ 2. ______ 3. ______ 4. ______ 5. ______ 6. ______

Actividad 9

There are advantages and disadvantages to choosing a career in art. As you listen to each statement, check off whether it describes an advantage (**ventaja**) or disadvantage (**desventaja**) of being in the art industry. You will hear each statement twice.

	1	2	3	4	5	6	7	8	9	10
Ventaja										
Desventaja										

Realidades 2 Nombre Hora

Capítulo 9A Fecha **WRITING**

Actividad 10

Your friend Carolina is visiting from Ecuador, and you have taken her to your neighborhood's annual summer party. Using the picture below, write complete sentences to tell her what each person at the party does for a living and what the job entails. Follow the model.

Modelo *Ella es diseñadora. Diseña y dibuja ropa de hombres y mujeres.*

A. ____________________

B. ____________________

C. ____________________

D. ____________________

E. ____________________

F. ____________________

G. ____________________

H. ____________________

I. ____________________

J. ____________________

Realidades 2 | Nombre ______ | Hora ______

Capítulo 9A | Fecha ______ | **WRITING**

Actividad 11

You and your friends are making predictions about what life will be like in the year 2100. Use your imagination to write complete sentences about the topics listed below. Follow the model.

Modelo los niños *A todos los niños les encantará ir a la escuela.*

1. los coches ______
2. la comida ______
3. los colègios ______
4. las casas ______
5. yo ______
6. nosotros ______
7. nuestro planeta ______
8. los Estados Unidos ______
9. mi familia ______
10. la ciudad de Nueva York ______

Realidades 2 | Nombre _______ | Hora _______

Capítulo 9A | Fecha _______ | WRITING

Actividad 12

Juanito is running for class president. Help him write his campaign promises about each topic by using the following verbs: **hacer, poder, saber, tener,** and **haber.** You may use each verb twice. Follow the model.

Modelo La escuela *tendrá tres cafeterías.*

1. Yo ____.
____
2. Los profesores ____.
____
3. El baile de la escuela ____.
____
4. Los estudiantes ____.
____
5. Mis mejores amigos y yo ____.
____
6. El día escolar ____.
____
7. La administración ____.
____
8. Nosotros ____.
____
9. La cafetería ____.
____
10. Los deportes ____.
____

Actividad 13

You are playing the fortune-teller at your school's winter carnival. Some of your friends want to find out what is going to happen to them in the future. Write at least three predictions for each of the people listed below. The first one has been started for you.

1. Nombre de un(a) amigo(a) ____________________

   Predicciones:

   Mi amigo tendrá una casa grande.

2. Nombre de dos amigos(as): ______________ y ______________

   Predicciones:

3. (Yo) Predicciones:

4. (Nosotros) Predicciones:

Realidades 2 | Nombre ______ | Hora ______

Capítulo 9B | Fecha ______ | VIDEO

Antes de ver el video

Actividad 1

Make a list of five things that can affect the environment or the Earth in general. One has been done for you.

1. *guerra*
2. ______
3. ______
4. ______
5. ______

¿Comprendes?

Actividad 2

Answer the following questions in order to better understand what happened in the video.

1. Pedro está en casa de Esteban. ¿Qué pasa?

______

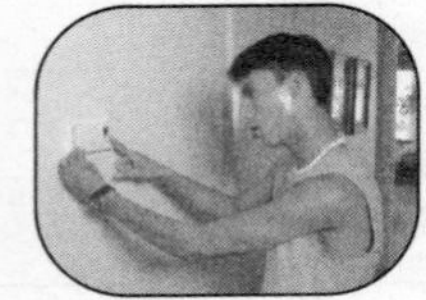

2. ¿Qué piensa Pedro?

______

3. Ellos tienen mucho calor. ¿Adónde deciden ir y por qué?

______

4. ¿De qué hablan Esteban y Pedro cuando van caminando al cine?

____

5. ¿A quién llama Esteban por el teléfono celular y para qué?

____

Actividad 3

Pedro and Esteban are talking about the good and bad effects things we use every day have on the environment. Write what each boy says about the following things.

Modelo **bicicleta**

Pedro: *reduce la contaminación y ahorra dinero*

Esteban: *el coche es más cómodo y más rápido*

1. **aire acondicionado solar**

   Pedro: ______________________

   Esteban: ______________________

2. **aire acondicionado**

   Pedro: ______________________

   Esteban: ______________________

3. **coche**

   Pedro: ______________________

   Esteban: ______________________

4. **autobús**

   Pedro: ______________________

   Esteban: ______________________

Actividad 4

Pedro has some good ideas about how to protect and preserve the environment but he cannot convince Esteban. Think about one way to protect and preserve the environment. Then, write three complete sentences to tell why your idea is important.

1. ______________________________

2. ______________________________

3. ______________________________

Actividad 5

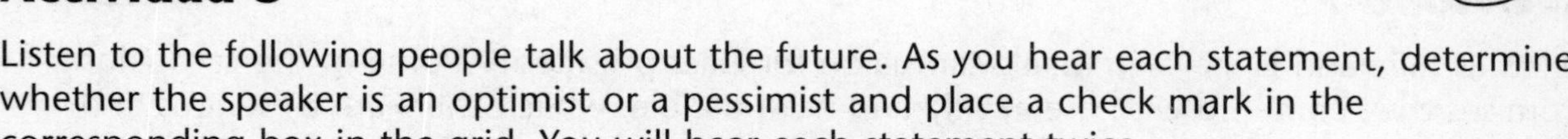

Listen to the following people talk about the future. As you hear each statement, determine whether the speaker is an optimist or a pessimist and place a check mark in the corresponding box in the grid. You will hear each statement twice.

	1	2	3	4	5	6	7	8
Optimista								
Pesimista								

Actividad 6

Listen as students in Sr. Naranjo's science class make predictions about the year 2020. As you hear each one, mark the number of the description underneath the picture it describes. Then, mark an X in the grid below to tell whether you agree with the prediction or doubt it will come true. Be prepared to tell why you answered the way you did. You will hear each prediction twice.

____

____

____

____

________ ________ ________

	1	2	3	4	5	6	7
Lo dudo							
Estoy de acuerdo							

Realidades 2 | Nombre ______ | Hora ______

Capítulo 9B | Fecha ______ | **AUDIO**

Actividad 7

Listen as Julia and Elena plan Julia's campaign for class president. Some of the campaign promises they come up with are a) silly and not possible, while others are b) serious and possible. As you listen to each idea, write **a** or **b** in the blanks provided. You will hear each statement twice.

1. ______ 2. ______ 3. ______ 4. ______ 5. ______ 6. ______ 7. ______ 8. ______

Actividad 8

The debate coach is observing a mock debate in order to determine whom she will select as partners (**compañeros**) for an upcoming debate on **"El futuro para nosotros."** Listen as the debaters answer the coach's questions. Fill in the chart below by circling each debater's opinion on the three issues. Which two people share the most opinions? You will hear each conversation twice.

	Las escuelas sin profesores	La paz mundial (*world peace*)	Vivir en la Luna
Ramón	Es posible Es imposible	Es posible Es imposible	Es posible Es imposible
Sandra	Es posible Es imposible	Es posible Es imposible	Es posible Es imposible
Lucas	Es posible Es imposible	Es posible Es imposible	Es posible Es imposible

¿Quiénes deben ser compañeros? ______________________________

Actividad 9

Listen to this class discussion about the problems in the world and solutions for a better world in the future. As you hear each comment, decide if the person is describing a problem or offering a solution. Place a check mark in the appropriate column in the grid below. You will hear each comment twice.

	1	2	3	4	5	6	7	8
Problema								
Solución								

Actividad 10

Look at the drawings below of environmental problems and their solutions. Describe how each one affects the environment. Write two complete sentences for each. Follow the model.

Modelo *Hay mucho humo que causa la contaminación del aire.*
Es un problema grave para el pueblo.

1. ____________________
____

2. ____________________
____

3. ____________________
____

4. ____________________
____

5. ____________________
____

6. ____________________
____

Actividad 11

The Valencia family is making plans to move to a new house. Look at the pictures below and tell what each person is planning, using the future tense of the verbs provided.

1.  yo (poner)

____.

2.  Marisa (querer)

____.

3. 

nosotros (salir)

____.

4.  mis amigos (venir)

____.

5.  yo (hacer)

____.

6. 

tú (decir)

____.

Actividad 12

Humberto is listening to the president's speech on the radio and is skeptical about what he hears. Read the excerpts below from the speech and write Humberto's reactions using phrases to express doubt. The first one has been done for you.

Los Estados Unidos deben ahorrar sus recursos naturales. Tendremos que conservar energía y reciclar para poder disfrutar una buena vida. Yo quiero reducir la contaminación del medio ambiente en los años que vienen...

También, quiero hacer planes para resolver nuestros conflictos internacionales. No podemos vivir si seguimos luchando entre países...

... Tenemos un problema con la economía. Les sugiero que los mejores economistas trabajen para mejorarla... Todos tienen que juntarse para proteger la Tierra... Mi plan puede funcionar si todos trabajamos juntos.

1. *Dudo que conservemos energía.*
2. ______
3. ______
4. ______
5. ______
6. ______
7. ______
8. ______

Actividad 13

You and your friends are proposing a plan to help preserve the environment, starting right in your own school.

A. Write a proposal to your school to launch your plan by listing five things you, your friends, and your school can do to make a difference. Use the future tense of some of the following verbs: **haber, hacer, poner, saber, decir, tener, venir, querer.** The first one has been done for you.

Tenemos que proteger nuestra Tierra. Por eso, nosotros haremos muchos cambios en nuestros hábitos:

- *Reciclaremos las latas y las botellas.*
-
-
-
-
-

B. Next, persuade the administration to accept your proposal by describing the environmental consequences of your plan. The description has been started for you.

Si seguimos este plan, veremos muchos cambios importantes. Es seguro que la Tierra mejorará. Dudamos que la destrucción continúe.

Notes

Notes

Notes

Notes

Notes

Notes

Notes

Notes

Notes

Notes

Notes

Notes

Notes

Notes

Test Preparation

Table of Contents

To the Student

Did you know that becoming a better reader in Spanish can improve your scores on standardized reading tests in English? Research has shown that the skills you develop by reading in a second language are transferred to reading in your first language. Research also shows that the more you practice for standardized tests and work on test-taking strategies, the more your scores will improve. The goal of this book is to help you improve your test-taking strategies and to provide extra practice with readings in both Spanish and English. For each chapter, you can work through three types of activities to improve your performance on tests: Reading Skills, Integrated Performance Assessments, and Practice Tests.

Reading Skills

The Reading Skills pages supplement the readings that appear in your textbook, giving you tools to become a better reader. Each Reading Skills page focuses on a specific strategy, such as determining the main idea or recognizing the use of comparison and contrast. After an explanation of the strategy, you'll find a tip for how to use it. Referring to a reading from your textbook, you'll put the reading tip into action by answering a practice question that may require you to fill out a graphic organizer or write a paragraph.

Finally, you'll answer a sample multiple-choice question that helps to prepare you to apply each strategy to reading comprehension questions on standardized tests.

Integrated Performance Assessments

In addition to written standardized tests, you may also be asked to demonstrate your abilities in Spanish by "integrating" your listening, reading, speaking, and writing skills into a "performance." The Integrated Performance Assessment pages contain a model for each chapter of what might be required.

The Integrated Performance Assessment for each chapter has three interrelated tasks for you to complete: the interpretive task, interpersonal task, and presentational task.

In the interpretive task, you will read a text, listen to an audio recording, or watch a video. Read, listen, or watch the piece once. Then, read the instructions for the interpersonal and presentational tasks. As you read, listen, or watch the piece for the second time, pay close attention to the elements you will need to complete the next two tasks, and take notes on anything you think may help you with them.

For the interpersonal task, you will work with a partner or a small group to discuss what you learned during the interpretive task. Before starting this task, scan the Interpretive Task Rubric to see how your work will be evaluated.

For the presentational task, you will take what you've learned in the interpretive and interpersonal tasks to create a formal presentation, whether written or spoken. Be sure to read the Presentational Task Rubric before starting so you will have an idea how your work will be assessed.

Practice Tests

The practice tests in this book offer a variety of readings to reflect the types of passages you might expect to find on a standardized test. They also provide practice for three different types of questions you are apt to encounter on such a test: multiple choice, Short Response, and Extended Response.

Multiple Choice Multiple choice questions always have four answer choices. Pick the one that is the best answer. A correct answer is worth 1 point.

Short Response This symbol appears next to questions requiring short written answers:

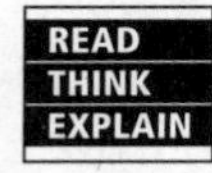

This symbol appears next to questions requiring short written answers that are a creative extension based on the reading:

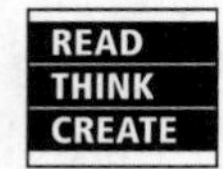

Take approximately 3 to 5 minutes to answer a Short Response question. Read all parts of the question carefully, plan your answer, then write the answer in your own words. A complete answer to a Short Response question is worth 2 points. A partial answer is worth 1 or 0 points.

NOTE: If a Short Response question is written in English, write your answer in English, unless the instructions tell you to do otherwise. If it is written in Spanish, write your answer in Spanish.

Extended Response This symbol appears next to questions requiring longer written answers based on information that can be inferred from the reading:

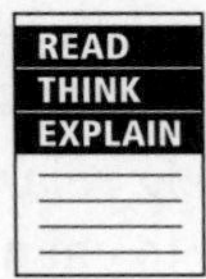

This symbol appears next to questions requiring longer written answers that are a creative extension based on the reading:

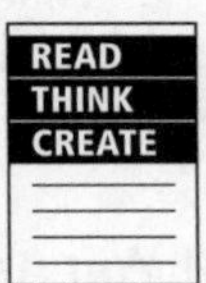

Take approximately 5 to 15 minutes to answer an Extended Response question. A complete answer is worth 4 points. A partial answer is worth 3, 2, 1, or 0 points.

NOTE: If an Extended Response question is written in English, write your answer in English. If it is written in Spanish, write your answer in Spanish.

Taking These Practice Tests

Your teacher will assign a test for classwork or homework, or you might be taking these tests on your own. Each reading is followed by questions, and the Response Sheet immediately follows the questions. For multiple choice questions, you should bubble-in the response. For Short and Extended Response questions, write your answers on the lines provided.

Tips for Improving Your Score

Know the Rules

Learn the rules for any test you take. For example, depending on how a test is scored, it may or may not be advisable to guess if you are not sure of the correct answer. Find that out before you begin the exam. Be sure you understand:

- how much time is allowed for the test
- the types of questions that will be asked
- how the questions should be answered
- how they will be scored

Know Yourself and Make a Plan

Ask yourself: "How will I prepare for the test?" First, ask your teacher to help you list your strengths and weaknesses on tests. Then make a detailed plan for practicing or reviewing. Give yourself plenty of time to prepare. Don't leave everything until the night before. Set aside blocks of uninterrupted time for studying, with short breaks at regular intervals.

Before the Test

Do something relaxing the night before. Then get a good night's sleep, and be sure to eat a nutritious meal before the test. Wear comfortable clothing. If possible, wear a watch or sit where you can see a clock. Make sure you have all the materials you will need. Find out in advance if you will need a certain type of pencil, for example, and bring several with you—already sharpened. Be sure you know where the test is being given and at what time. Plan to arrive early.

Know What You Are Being Asked

There are two basic types of test questions: objective, one-right-answer questions and essay questions. It is essential that you read <u>all</u> questions carefully. Ask yourself, "What are they asking me?" The purpose of a standardized reading test is to determine:

- how well you understand what you read
- how well you are able to use the critical thinking and problem-solving skills that are so critical for success in today's world

Here is a list of basic reading skills:

- Understanding major ideas, details, and organization
- Drawing conclusions
- Understanding cause and effect
- Comparing and contrasting
- Finding, interpreting, and organizing information
- Understanding author's purpose and/or viewpoint
- Understanding character and plot development

Always read the questions <u>before</u> you read the passage. This will help you focus on the task. If it is allowed, ask your teacher to explain any directions you do not understand.

Watch Your Time

Allot a specific amount of time per question—approximately 1 minute for multiple choice, 3 to 5 minutes for Short Response, and 5 to 15 minutes for Extended Response. Do not spend too much time on any one question, and monitor your time so that you will be able to complete the test.

Show What You Know, Relax, and Think Positively

Answer those questions that you are sure about first. If a question seems too difficult, skip it and return to it later. Remember that while some questions may seem hard, others will be easy. You may never learn to love taking tests, but you can control the situation and make sure that you reach your full potential for success.

Above all, relax. It's natural to be nervous, but think positively. Just do your best.

Multiple Choice Questions: Helpful Hints

Multiple choice questions have only one right answer. There is no "creative" response, only a correct one. This book provides extensive practice for the types of multiple choice items that you might find on a standardized reading test. There are four answer choices (A, B, C, D or F, G, H, J) per question. Allot approximately 1 minute to answer a multiple choice question. Answers are worth 1 point each.

- Read the question carefully.
- Try to identify the answer before you examine the choices.
- Eliminate obviously incorrect choices by lightly crossing them out.
- Try to narrow the choices down to two.
- Depending on how a test is to be scored, you may or may not want to guess (for these practice tests, check that you will **not** be penalized for guessing wrong).

Short and Extended Response: Helpful Hints

The dreaded essay question will probably not be as difficult as expected if you follow these strategies:

- Read the question before reading the passage.
- Re-read the question as you prepare to respond: Are you being asked to list, describe, explain, discuss, persuade, or compare and contrast? These are very different things.
- Look back at the passage as often as necessary to answer the question correctly. Underline any key sections that you think might be important to your response.
- Use the margins next to the passage to jot down thoughts and ideas and to prepare a brief outline of what you will include in your answer. Use a clear, direct introduction that answers the specific question being asked. As a start, try turning the question into a statement. Include both general ideas and specific details from the reading in your answer.
- Review your response to make sure you have expressed your thoughts well. Is your introduction clear? Have you stated the general idea(s)? Have you included supporting details?

- If your response is in Spanish, check for grammar errors (subject-verb agreement, adjective agreement, correct verb endings and tenses). In either language, proofread your answer for correct spelling.

How the Test Will Be Scored

It is important to know in advance how responses will be scored. This will lower your anxiety level and help you focus. For the purpose of these practice tests, you can assume the following:

Multiple Choice Questions

Multiple choice answers are either right or wrong. You will receive credit and 1 point if you select the correct answer.

Performance-Based Questions (Short and Extended Response)

Short and Extended Response questions are called "performance tasks." They are often scored with rubrics, which describe a range of performance. You will receive credit for how close your answers come to the desired response. The performance tasks on these practice tests will require thoughtful answers. You must:

- Read the passage
- Think about the question as it relates to the passage, and
- Explain your answer by citing general ideas and specific details from the passage

or:

- Create a written document (a letter, for example) that clearly uses or models information provided in the reading passage

Rubric for Short Response Questions

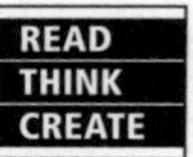

2 points The response indicates that the student has a complete understanding of the reading concept embodied in the task. The student has provided a response that is accurate, complete, and fulfills all the requirements of the task. Necessary support and/or examples are included, and the information given is clearly text-based. Any extensions beyond the text are relevant to the task.

1 point The response indicates that the student has a partial understanding of the reading concept embodied in the task. The student has provided a response that may include information that is essentially correct and text-based, but the information is too general or too simplistic. Some of the support and/or examples may be incomplete or omitted.

0 points The response is inaccurate, confused, and/or irrelevant, or the student has failed to respond to the task.

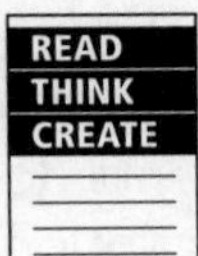

Rubric for Extended Response Questions

4 points The response indicates that the student has a thorough understanding of the reading concept embodied in the task. The student has provided a response that is accurate, complete, and fulfills all the requirements of the task. Necessary support and/or examples are included, and the information given is clearly text-based. Any extensions beyond the text are relevant to the task.

3 points The response indicates that the student has an understanding of the reading concept embodied in the task. The student has provided a response that is accurate and fulfills all the requirements of the task, but the required support and/or details are not complete or clearly text-based.

2 points The response indicates that the student has a partial understanding of the reading concept embodied in the task. The student has provided a response that may include information that is essentially correct and text-based, but the information is too general or too simplistic. Some of the support and/or examples and requirements of the task may be incomplete or omitted.

1 point The response indicates that the student has very limited understanding of the reading concept embodied in the task. The response is incomplete, may exhibit many flaws, and may not address all requirements of the task.

0 points The response is inaccurate, confused, and/or irrelevant, or the student has failed to respond to the task.

Getting Started

So let's get started. If there was anything in this Introduction that you did not understand, ask your teacher about it. Glance once again at the Helpful Hints before taking the first test. In fact, it will be helpful if you review those hints each time you take one of these tests. And remember: The more you practice, the higher your scores will be.

¡Buena suerte!

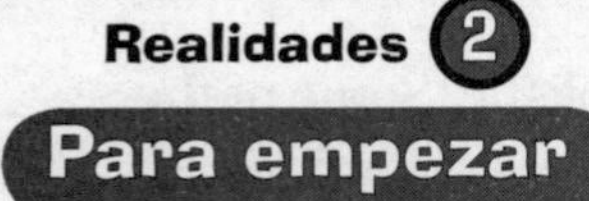

Integrated Performance Assessment
Unit theme: ¿Cómo eres tú?, ¿Qué haces?

Context for the Integrated Performance Assessment: You are going to spend a week in Mexico with a group of exchange students. Your host student is looking forward to meeting you. He/she wants to know what you are like and some of your favorite activities.

Interpretive Task: Listen to several students as they describe themselves on *Realidades 2, Audio Program DVD: Cap. PE, Track 3.* (Don't worry about the directions given on the DVD itself. Use these directions instead.) As you listen, pay attention to how students describe themselves and what activities they like and don't like to do. Write down the descriptions that fit you and the activities that you like or do not like to do.

Interpretive Task: Work with a friend in Spanish class. Tell your friend about yourself using the description and activities that you wrote down. Listen to your friend's description. Ask each other questions to learn more about what you are like and what you like and do not like to do.

Presentational Task: Write an e-mail to your host student in Mexico introducing yourself. Tell him/her what you are like and the activities you like and do not like to do.

Interpersonal Task Rubric

	Score: 1 Does not meet expectations	**Score: 3 Meets expectations**	**Score: 5 Exceeds expectations**
Language Use	Student uses little or no target language and relies heavily on native language word order.	Student uses the target language consistently, but may mix native and target language word order.	Student uses the target language exclusively and integrates target language word order into conversation.
Vocabulary Use	Student uses limited and repetitive language.	Student uses only recently acquired vocabulary.	Student uses both recently and previously acquired vocabulary.

Presentational Task Rubric

	Score: 1 Does not meet expectations	**Score: 3 Meets expectations**	**Score: 5 Exceeds expectations**
Amount of Communication	Student gives limited or no details or examples.	Student gives adequate details or examples.	Student gives consistent details or examples.
Accuracy	Student's accuracy with vocabulary and structures is limited.	Student's accuracy with vocabulary and structures is adequate.	Student's accuracy with vocabulary and structures is exemplary.
Comprehensibility	Student's ideas lack clarity and are difficult to understand.	Student's ideas are adequately clear and fairly well understood.	Student's ideas are precise and easily understood.
Vocabulary Use	Student uses limited and repetitive vocabulary.	Student uses only recently acquired vocabulary.	Student uses both recently and previously acquired vocabulary.

Reading Skills: Actividad 9, p. 25

Recognizing the Use of Comparison and Contrast

To recognize comparison and contrast in a reading passage, good readers can point out how items or ideas in the reading passage are similar to or different from each other. Sometimes writers will directly state that they are comparing or contrasting items in a reading passage. Other times readers might recognize items in a reading passage that could be compared or contrasted even though the writer might not have presented the information for that purpose.

Tip

The Venn diagram is an excellent visual tool to help students see differences and similarities when comparing and contrasting. The area where two circles overlap is the place to list the similarities between items. List the differences between items in the areas that do not overlap.

1. On page 25 in your textbook, re-read the poem *"Versos sencillos"* in **Actividad 9.** After you have finished reading, complete the Venn diagram below to show the similarities and differences in the way that the speaker treats and is treated by his friends and enemies.

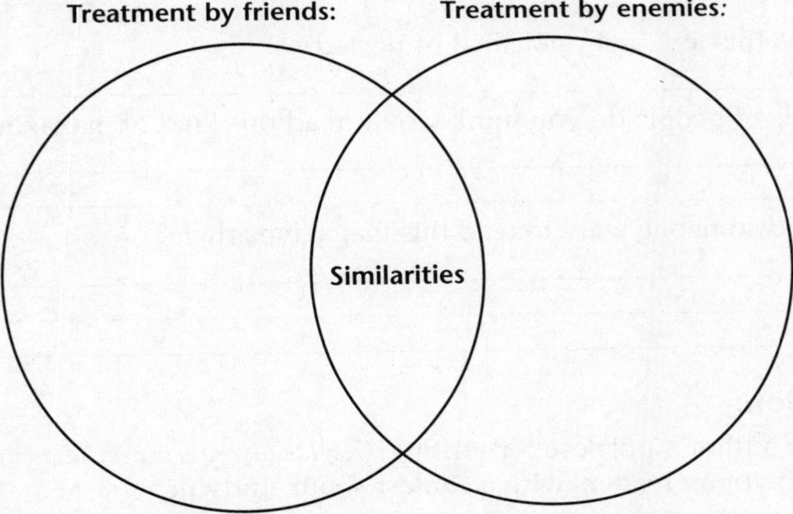

Sample question:

2. What is most surprising about the poem *"Versos sencillos"*?
   - **A** The speaker's enemies tear out his heart.
   - **B** The speaker's friends are sincere in offering a hand.
   - **C** The speaker treats both his friends and enemies the same way.
   - **D** The speaker's enemies treat him the same way that his friends do.

Realidades 2 Nombre _______________ Fecha _______________

Capítulo 1A

Reading Skills: Lectura, pp. 34–35
Fondo Cultural, p. 35

Determining the Author's Purpose

To determine the author's purpose for writing a book, a story, an article, or any other text, the reader must figure out why the author wrote that particular book, story, article, or text. Some common purposes for writing are to inform, to entertain, to persuade, or to describe. Readers should also be able to explain why the author uses different techniques or includes different features within a text.

Tip

To figure out the author's purpose, ask yourself these questions:

- Where was this text first published or posted?
- What kinds of people would read this kind of newsletter, advertisement, pamphlet, book, magazine, Web site, text, etc.?
- Why would someone want to read this newsletter, advertisement, pamphlet, book, magazine, Web site, text, etc.?

1. On pages 34 and 35 in your textbook, re-read the **Lectura,** ***Para estudiar mejor...*** and the **Fondo cultural** about the Spanish magazine *Okapi*. Then answer the following questions about the text *"Reglas de oro para estudiar mejor."*

Where was this text first published or posted?

____

What kinds of people do you think would read this kind of magazine?

____

____

Why would someone want to read this magazine article?

____

____

____

Sample question:

2. What was the author's purpose for writing *"Reglas de oro para estudiar mejor"*?

A to entertain young readers with a contest about studying
B to persuade readers to improve their study skills
C to tell a story about a student who became a success after improving his study skills
D to explain how young readers can improve their study habits

Realidades 2

Capítulo 1A

Integrated Performance Assessment

Unit theme: ¿Qué haces en la escuela?

Context for the Integrated Performance Assessment: A group of students from Mexico is coming to spend three weeks in your school and attend classes with you. They want to make a very good impression, so they would like to know some of the class and school rules.

Interpretive Task: Listen to several teachers as they describe their class rules. Take notes on the rules you hear that you have to follow in your classes from *Realidades 2, Audio Program DVD: Cap. 1A, Track 6.* (Don't worry about the directions given on the DVD itself. Use these directions instead.)

Interpretive Task: Work with a group of 2 or 3 students. Talk about the rules in your classes and listen to the other students talk about the rules in their classes. Then discuss some school-wide rules until your group has identified 2 or 3. Take additional notes.

Presentational Task: Using your notes, write an e-mail to one of the students from Mexico explaining the class and school rules that he/she will have to follow when he/she comes to your school.

Interpersonal Task Rubric

	Score: 1 Does not meet expectations	Score: 3 Meets expectations	Score: 5 Exceeds expectations
Language Use	Student uses little or no target language and relies heavily on native language word order.	Student uses the target language consistently, but may mix native and target language word order.	Student uses the target language exclusively and integrates target language word order into conversation.
Vocabulary Use	Student uses limited and repetitive language.	Student uses only recently acquired vocabulary.	Student uses both recently and previously acquired vocabulary.

Presentational Task Rubric

	Score: 1 Does not meet expectations	Score: 3 Meets expectations	Score: 5 Exceeds expectations
Amount of Communication	Student gives limited or no details or examples.	Student gives adequate details or examples.	Student gives consistent details or examples.
Accuracy	Student's accuracy with vocabulary and structures is limited.	Student's accuracy with vocabulary and structures is adequate.	Student's accuracy with vocabulary and structures is exemplary.
Comprehensibility	Student's ideas lack clarity and are difficult to understand.	Student's ideas are adequately clear and fairly well understood.	Student's ideas are precise and easily understood.
Vocabulary Use	Student uses limited and repetitive vocabulary.	Student uses only recently acquired vocabulary.	Student uses both recently and previously acquired vocabulary.

 Reading Skills: Actividad 23, p. 61

Determining the Author's Purpose

To determine the author's purpose for writing a book, a story, an article, or any other text, the reader must figure out why the author wrote that particular book, story, article, or text. Some common purposes for writing are to inform, to entertain, to persuade, or to describe.

Readers should also be able to explain why the author uses different techniques or includes different features within a text. Readers familiar with this skill understand that authors compose texts deliberately, making purposeful decisions about which words, sentence constructions, and organization patterns are most effective in communicating a message.

Tip

Once readers can determine the author's overall purpose for composing a text, they pay attention to how different features in the text help achieve that purpose. Word choice is one common feature for you to examine to find the author's purpose for writing. In examining the author's word choice, you should consider how different choices of words could change the effect the text has on a reader.

1. On page 61 in your textbook, re-read **Actividad 23**, brochure for the *Club Deportivo Acuasol*. Answer the questions that follow.

What is the author's overall purpose for writing the brochure for *Club Deportivo Acuasol*?

____

____

What effect would the following changes in wording in the brochure have on readers?

(Original) Tenemos una misión: dar a nuestra comunidad un lugar agradable para el ejercicio personal y la integración de la familia, a través del deporte...
(Change) Tenemos una misión: dar un lugar agradable para el ejercicio personal...
Effect: ______________________________

____

(Original) Hay una variedad de cursos tanto culturales como deportivos, en diferentes horarios...
(Change) Hay una variedad de cursos deportivos en diferentes horarios...
Effect: ______________________________

____

Sample question:

2. Which technique used in the brochure does NOT help the author achieve his or her purpose of portraying *Club Deportivo Acuasol* as a different kind of athletic club?

A A list of activities offered at the club includes regional dance and tai chi chuan.
B The club is described as an agreeable place for personal exercise.
C The club's mission includes mention of family togetherness.
D The club is described as a place to broaden one's cultural and social horizons.

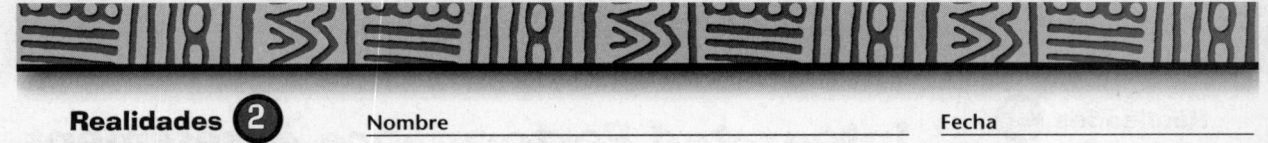

Reading Skills: Lectura pp. 62–63

Locates, Gathers, Analyzes, and Evaluates Written Information

By showing that they can locate, gather, analyze, and evaluate information from one or more reading passages, good readers demonstrate that they know how to conduct research. On a test, readers are often asked to locate, gather, analyze, and evaluate information from a reading passage and then show how to put that information to good use.

Tip

Readers who conduct research often read with a purpose. That means that you should have a research question or problem in your head while you read. If you encounter information in a reading passage that relates to your research question or problem, you should underline or highlight that information. Later, you should come back to the sections that you highlighted to analyze and evaluate the information to determine if it will be useful for your research.

1. On pages 62–63 in your textbook, re-read the **Lectura,** ***¡A bailar!*** After you finish reading, consider the following scenario:

   Imagine that a scholarship organization in your community will pay the fees for young people to get involved in cultural organizations such as *La escuela internacional de baile.* Interested young people need only submit a letter in which they explain how the scholarship will benefit them. Now, with a pencil, pen, or highlighter, underline the information from the **Lectura** below that might be useful to include in your letter.

   La escuela de baile te ofrece una gran variedad de clases de bailes tradicionales y contemporáneos. Puedes participar en una actividad sana y deportiva que te ayuda a entender las ricas tradiciones y costumbres de varios países hispanohablantes.

   Flamenco–Aprende los pasos importantes de este misterioso baile de Andalucía. Swing–Baila toda la noche con tu pareja este baile muy popular de los Estados Unidos.

   Then, explain how the information you underlined could help you persuade the scholarship organization to pay your fees at *La escuela internacional de baile.*

   ____

   ____

   ____

   ____

Sample question:

2. Which detail from the **Lectura** would be most effective in persuading a scholarship organization to pay your fees at *La escuela internacional de baile*?
   - **A** You can dance swing all night with your partner.
   - **B** You can win a lot of prizes.
   - **C** You can better understand the rich traditions and customs of Spanish-speaking countries.
   - **D** You can impress your friends by moving your hips to the rhythm of *merengue.*

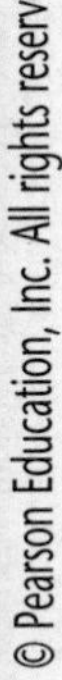

Realidades 2

Capítulo 1B

Integrated Performance Assessment
Unit theme: ¿Qué haces después de las clases?

Context for the Integrated Performance Assessment: The Spanish Club at your school is preparing for the arrival of a group of exchange students from Spain. You are on the committee that is going to make a presentation on your school's extracurricular program to the students. Since the students do not have many extracurricular activities at their school they are really looking forward to participating in some at your school.

Interpretive Task: Watch the *Videohistoria: Después de las clases* from *Realidades 2, DVD 1, Capítulo 1B* where several students talk about extracurricular activities at their school in Texas. As you watch the video, make a list of the activities at their school.

Interpersonal Task: Compare your list of activities from the video with the lists of the other members of the committee, adding activities that are offered at your own school. Discuss which extracurricular activities you think would be interesting for the Spanish students, and select a variety to present to them. Include a description of what students do during the activities you select and how much time each activity takes.

Presentational Task: Make an oral presentation to the students from Spain telling them about a variety of extracurricular activities at your school. Describe each activity and tell them how much time each activity takes.

Interpersonal Task Rubric

	Score: 1 Does not meet expectations	Score: 3 Meets expectations	Score: 5 Exceeds expectations
Language Use	Student uses little or no target language and relies heavily on native language word order.	Student uses the target language consistently, but may mix native and target language word order.	Student uses the target language exclusively and integrates target language word order into conversation.
Vocabulary Use	Student uses limited and repetitive language.	Student uses only recently acquired vocabulary.	Student uses both recently and previously acquired vocabulary.

Presentational Task Rubric

	Score: 1 Does not meet expectations	Score: 3 Meets expectations	Score: 5 Exceeds expectations
Amount of Communication	Student gives limited or no details or examples.	Student gives adequate details or examples.	Student gives consistent details or examples.
Accuracy	Student's accuracy with vocabulary and structures is limited.	Student's accuracy with vocabulary and structures is adequate.	Student's accuracy with vocabulary and structures is exemplary.
Comprehensibility	Student's ideas lack clarity and are difficult to understand.	Student's ideas are adequately clear and fairly well understood.	Student's ideas are precise and easily understood.
Vocabulary Use	Student uses limited and repetitive vocabulary.	Student uses only recently acquired vocabulary.	Student uses both recently and previously acquired vocabulary.

Practice Test

¿Por qué está tan *nervioso*?

1 Son las seis y media de la mañana y Marcos está preparándose para el primer día de clases en su nueva escuela. Decide llevar sus jeans nuevos y una camiseta negra.

—Buenos días, Marcos.

—Buenos días, mamá.

—¿Cómo estás?

—Estoy un poco nervioso, mamá.

—¿Por qué? Todo va a estar bien. ¿Tienes todo lo que necesitas en tu mochila?

—Sí, tengo dos bolígrafos, cuatro lápices, un cuaderno, una carpeta de argollas, una calculadora y un diccionario.

—Eres muy ordenado, hijo. Pues, es la hora de salir para la escuela.

2 Cuando Marcos entra en la sala de clases para su clase de primera hora, una estudiante le dice:

—Hola. Me llamo Carolina. ¿Y tú?

—Me llamo Marcos.

—Mucho gusto, Marcos.

—Igualmente, Carolina. ¿De dónde eres?

—Soy de Panamá. ¿Y tú?

—Soy de Perú.

—¿Qué clases tienes?

—Tengo álgebra, historia, español, inglés, biología, literatura, educación física y arte.

—¿A qué hora tienes el almuerzo, Marcos?

—En la cuarta hora.

—Yo también. Pues, ¿te gustaría comer el almuerzo conmigo y con algunos de mis amigos? La cafetería tiene una buena selección de ensaladas y toda clase de sándwiches.

—Sí, me gustaría mucho.

3 Después de su clase de tercera hora, Marcos entra en la cafetería donde están Carolina y sus amigos, Ramón, Javier, María, David y Linda. Todos hablan sobre sus clases y sus actividades extracurriculares. Ramón es miembro de la banda y toca el saxofón. También juega al béisbol. Javier juega al fútbol americano y practica artes marciales. María hace gimnasia y también es bailarina. David juega al básquetbol y trabaja en un supermercado. Linda juega al fútbol y es presidenta del consejo estudiantil. Y Carolina escribe para la revista literaria, canta en el coro y juega al vóleibol.

—Marcos, ¿qué actividades te interesan más? —le pregunta Ramón.

—Pues, toco la trompeta y me gustaría ser miembro de la banda. También me encanta jugar al tenis. ¿Tienen un equipo de tenis en esta escuela?

—¡Claro que sí! Y es uno de los mejores equipos de tenis de nuestra división —le responde Linda.

—Mañana a las tres de la tarde, hay una reunión en el auditorio donde se puede aprender más sobre todas las actividades extracurriculares de la escuela. ¿Por qué no vienes con nosotros? —le dice Javier.

—Bueno. Voy a estar allí.

—Entonces mañana todos nosotros vamos a comer el almuerzo y después de las clases vamos a la reunión —dice David.

Cuando terminan de comer el almuerzo, todos dicen "adiós" y salen para llegar a tiempo a su próxima clase.

4 Cuando Marcos regresa a casa, está cansado pero muy contento porque a él le gusta mucho su nueva escuela. También le gustan sus nuevos compañeros de clase. Quiere participar en unas de las actividades extracurriculares de su escuela y también se interesa en trabajar como tutor en álgebra.

Realidades 2

Tema 1 **Practice Test**

Answer questions 1—6. Base your answers on the reading, *"¿Por qué está tan nervioso?"*.

1 Why is Marcos so nervous?

- **A** He has lost his class schedule.
- **B** It's his first day at a new school.
- **C** He can't find his backpack.
- **D** He doesn't have all of his school supplies.

2 According to the story, what happens when Marcos arrives at school?

- **F** He has breakfast in the cafeteria.
- **G** He realizes that he's forgotten his backpack.
- **H** A classmate introduces herself to him.
- **J** He realizes that he's late for class.

3 What was discussed during Marcos's lunch with Carolina and her friends?

- **A** their classes and extracurricular activities
- **B** their favorite musical instruments
- **C** their favorite foods
- **D** the meeting that was held to discuss school activities

4 How does Marcos feel at the end of the day?

- **F** He's tired from playing tennis.
- **G** He's happy because the students are friendly and the school has a lot to offer.
- **H** He's happy because he has a student to tutor in algebra.
- **J** He's happy because he has signed up for band and the tennis team.

5 READ THINK EXPLAIN ¿Cómo son los nuevos amigos de Marcos?

6 

Imagina que eres un(a) nuevo(a) estudiante en tu escuela. Haz una lista de todo lo que debes hacer para tener un primer día perfecto.

Realidades 2

Nombre ______________________ Fecha ____________

Tema 1

Practice Test Answer Sheet

1 Ⓐ Ⓑ Ⓒ Ⓓ   2 Ⓕ Ⓖ Ⓗ Ⓙ   3 Ⓐ Ⓑ Ⓒ Ⓓ

4 Ⓕ Ⓖ Ⓗ Ⓙ

5

READ
THINK
EXPLAIN

6

READ
THINK
EXPLAIN

Realidades 2 Nombre ____________ Fecha ____________

Capítulo 2A **Reading Skills: Conexiones, p. 83**

Determining the Main Idea

To determine the main idea of reading passage, the reader must be able to describe what a reading passage is mostly about. He or she should be able to summarize the main idea of a reading passage in one sentence. A common problem when working with this skill is confusing an important detail in the reading passage for the main idea. Just because something is mentioned in the reading passage does not mean it is the main idea of the passage. Many times the main idea is not even stated in the reading passage. This is often called an implied main idea. No matter if the main idea is stated or implied, the basic question remains the same: "What is this reading passage mostly about?"

Tip

Readers are more likely to understand a reading passage when it deals with a topic with which the reader is already familiar. This familiarity with a topic is known as the reader's prior knowledge. Activating your prior knowledge before reading is one way to improve your understanding of a reading passage, and one popular method of activating your prior knowledge is a **K-W-L** chart.

1. Before reading the **Conexiones,** ***¿Necesitas dormir más?*** on page 83 in the your textbook, complete the **K** and **W** portions of the chart. After you have written your responses, share them with a classmate. After reading ***¿Necesitas dormir más?*** complete the **L** portion of the chart.

K **What I Already Know**	**W** **What I Want to Know**	**L** **What I Learned from Reading**
List 3 things you already know about the topic of sleep. Even if your memory is fuzzy or facts are wrong, try to write something.	*List 3 things that you would like to know about the topic of sleep. Even if that topic does not personally interest you, try to write something.*	*List 2 important details that you learned from your reading of the article on page 83* ¿Necesitas dormir más? *Then state in one sentence what the article is mostly about.*
1. ____________	**1.** ____________	**1.** ____________
2. ____________	**2.** ____________	**2.** ____________
3. ____________	**3.** ____________	**3.** This passage was mostly about ____________

Sample question:

2. What is the main idea of the article ***¿Necesitas dormir más?***
   - **A** Young people are not sleeping enough, but this situation could be improved.
   - **B** Do not exercise right before you go to bed.
   - **C** Young people need to sleep 1.25 hours more than adults.
   - **D** Poor sleeping habits affect people of all ages, from infants to senior citizens.

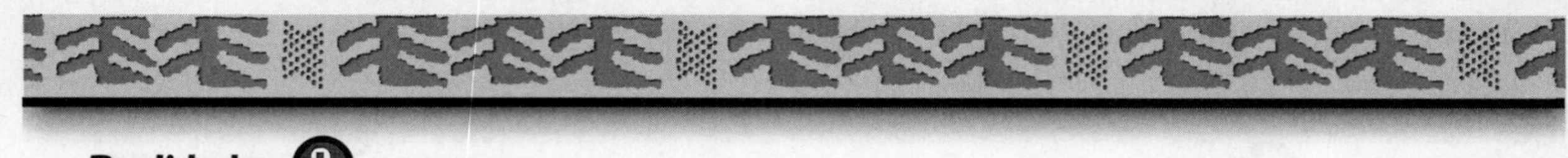

Realidades 2 | Nombre ______ Fecha ______

Capítulo 2A

Reading Skills: Lectura, pp. 90–91

Drawing Conclusions

To draw a conclusion is to form an opinion based on evidence. If you watch television crime shows, then you have seen detectives analyze a crime scene to form an opinion or draw a conclusion. Readers are often asked to draw conclusions about what they have read. This task often asks readers to determine if there is enough evidence present in the text to support a certain conclusion.

Conclusion statements are rarely simply right or wrong. They are often presented as believable or not and conclusions are only as strong as the evidence on which they are based. If you are successful at drawing conclusions from your reading, then you are likely skilled at finding evidence that supports your conclusions.

Tip

One strategy that helps students as they draw conclusions is a two-column note activity known as Opinion-Proof. As you read, you formulate opinions about what you have read. You write these on the Opinion side of your notes. If your opinions are believable, then you should be able to write down on the Proof side all the evidence you find in the reading passage that lends support to your opinion.

1. On pages 90–91 in your textbook, re-read the **Lectura,** ***El Teatro Colón: Entre bambalinas***. Based on what you have read, fill in the Opinion-Proof chart below.

Opinion	Proof
There are a lot of ways to become part of an artistic group at the Teatro Colón.	______
______	*El Teatro Colón lleva casi 150 años ofreciendo ópera al público argentino.*

Sample question:

2. Based on the **Lectura,** ***El Teatro Colón: Entre bambalinas,*** which conclusion below is the most believable?
   - **A** The Argentinian people prefer tango over opera at the Colón Theater.
   - **B** If you are interested in technology, you will not find a place to get involved at the Colón Theater.
   - **C** The Colón Theater has played an important role in the lives of many citizens of Buenos Aires.
   - **D** Auditioning is the hardest part about working at the Colón Theater.

Realidades 2

Capítulo 2A

Integrated Performance Assessment
Unit theme: ¿Cómo te preparas?

Context for the Integrated Performance Assessment: A group of students from Colombia is coming to spend three weeks in your high school. Your Spanish teacher would like you to host one of the students but you need some additional information before you make a decision.

Interpretive Task: Your Spanish teacher thinks you would be a good match for one of 6 students. Listen to each of the 6 students as they talk about an upcoming event in their lives on *Realidades 2, Audio Program DVD: Cap. 2A, Track 7.* (Don't worry about the directions given on the DVD itself. Use these directions instead.) The upcoming event gives you a good idea of the interests of each student. As you listen, write down the name of each student and the event he/she describes. Select the student that is the best match for you.

Interpersonal Task: Work with a friend in Spanish class. Tell your friend the name of the student you have selected and explain why. Tell your friend that you need more information about the student's daily routines to know if he/she is really a good match. Work with your friend to prepare a list of questions to ask about the student's daily routines.

Presentational Task: Write a note to your teacher giving him/her the name of the student you have selected and explain why. Tell your teacher that you would like more information about the student, especially about the student's daily routines. Ask your teacher several questions in order to get the additional information.

Interpersonal Task Rubric

	Score: 1 Does not meet expectations	Score: 3 Meets expectations	Score: 5 Exceeds expectations
Language Use	Student uses little or no target language and relies heavily on native language word order.	Student uses the target language consistently, but may mix native and target language word order.	Student uses the target language exclusively and integrates target language word order into conversation.
Vocabulary Use	Student uses limited and repetitive language.	Student uses only recently acquired vocabulary.	Student uses both recently and previously acquired vocabulary.

Presentational Task Rubric

	Score: 1 Does not meet expectations	Score: 3 Meets expectations	Score: 5 Exceeds expectations
Amount of Communication	Student gives limited or no details or examples.	Student gives adequate details or examples.	Student gives consistent details or examples.
Accuracy	Student's accuracy with vocabulary and structures is limited.	Student's accuracy with vocabulary and structures is adequate.	Student's accuracy with vocabulary and structures is exemplary.
Comprehensibility	Student's ideas lack clarity and are difficult to understand.	Student's ideas are adequately clear and fairly well understood.	Student's ideas are precise and easily understood.
Vocabulary Use	Student uses limited and repetitive vocabulary.	Student uses only recently acquired vocabulary.	Student uses both recently and previously acquired vocabulary.

Realidades 2 Nombre ______ Fecha ______

Capítulo 2B

Reading Skills: Actividad 18, pp. 112–113

Recognizing Cause-Effect Relationships

To recognize cause-effect relationships in fiction, nonfiction, drama, or poetry, readers should be aware of why things happen (causes) as well as the consequences or results of actions (effects) in a reading passage.

Tip

To become familiar with this skill, you should be able to identify certain words or phrases that are often used to show cause-effect relationships. You should also be able to use these words or phrases to describe what you have read in a reading passage. Here are some common cause-effect words or phrases (grouped by similarity in meaning):

because	as a result
due to	hence
as a result of	thus
since	consequently
so that	therefore

1. On pages 112 and 113 in your textbook, re-read **Actividad 18** ***"Los textiles y el cuero."*** After you have finished reading, complete the sentences below.

______________________________;
consequently, the Native Americans incorporated sheep's wool into their traditional fabrics.

Because Eli Whitney invented the cotton gin, ______________________________.

With the mechanical advances and inventions of the Industrial Revolution, production increased. **As a result,** ______________________________.

Due to scientific methods, electronics, and computers, ______________________________.

Sample question:

2. Based on your reading of the timeline *"La historia"* on page 112, which statement below is true?

A Because the Spanish explorers brought the loom to America, Native Americans learned to weave.

B Because of scientific advances from the Industrial Revolution, Argentina and Brazil became world leaders in the production of leather.

C Because of the cotton gin, Lowell, Massachusetts, was home to the first textile factory.

D Because the Spanish brought sheep to the Americas, Native Americans incorporated wool into their traditional fabrics.

Reading Skills: Lectura, pp.118–119

Identifying Methods of Development and Patterns of Organization

Good readers understand the tools and techniques of authors. To identify the methods of development used by an author in a text, good readers must first determine the author's purpose by asking, "Why was this text written?" After determining the author's purpose, readers next ask, "What techniques did the author use to achieve his or her purpose?" These techniques are known as methods of development and could include, among other things, the organization pattern, the word choice, or the sentence structure used in the text.

Tip

One common pattern of organization for writers is the process paper. The process paper could be a set of instructions, the summary of a story, a "how-to" guide, or even a recipe. In a process paper, you explain the steps in a process. A graphic organizer known as a flow chart helps you keep track of all these steps. The flow chart also helps you see which steps come first in the process and which ones follow.

1. Review the **Lectura, *Los jeans*** on pages 118 and 119 in your textbook. After re-reading the section *"Un poco de historia,"* fill in the flow chart below with the steps that led Levi Strauss from being an immigrant to America to becoming one of the world's best known inventors.

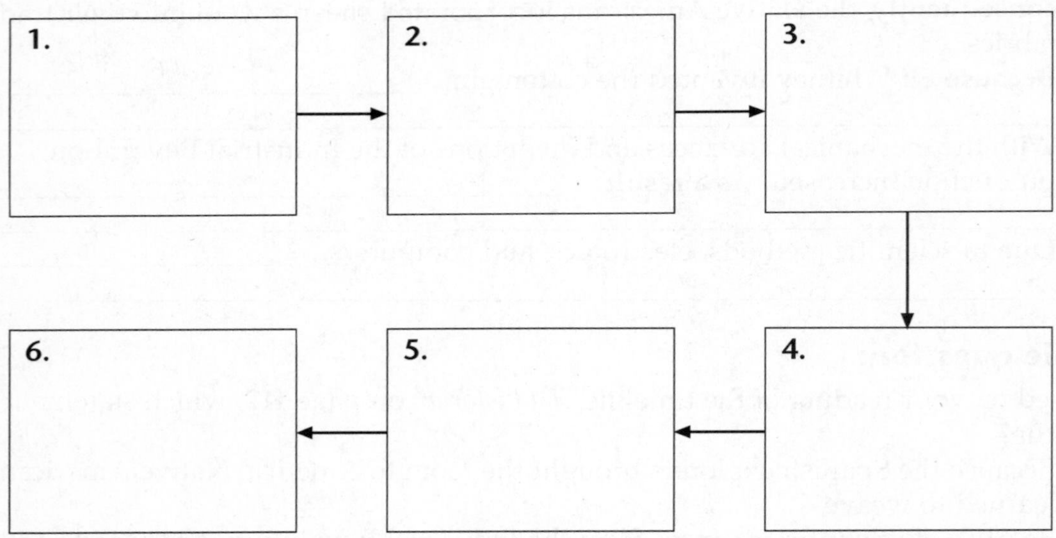

Sample question:

2. According to the **Lectura, *Los jeans,*** what happened before Levi Strauss learned how to place rivets in the corners of men's pants pockets?
   A He applied for a patent for the riveting process.
   B He already was a successful seller of clothing in California.
   C Jeans had become one of the most popular kinds of pants in the world.
   D He and his family were almost bankrupt.

Realidades 2

Capítulo 2B

Integrated Performance Assessment

Unit theme: ¿Qué ropa compraste?

Context for the Integrated Performance Task: A group of students from Costa Rica is coming to spend time in your community. Due to new luggage restrictions imposed by the airlines, each student can only bring one small suitcase and will need to shop for more clothes. They are especially concerned about the Homecoming Dance that takes place shortly after they arrive and have asked you to give them some shopping suggestions.

Interpretive Task: Watch the *Videohistoria: Buscando una ganga* from *Realidades 2, DVD 1, Capítulo 2B* where students go shopping in Costa Rica. Notice what interests them and what they buy.

Interpersonal Task: In a group of 3 or 4, talk about the clothes the students should have for school, for weekend activities, and for the Homecoming Dance. Make a list of stores where the students can shop and can find good prices.

Presentational Task: Prepare a detailed shopping guide for the students that gives the names of stores, the kinds of clothes they can find in each store, and information about prices.

Interpersonal Task Rubric

	Score: 1 Does not meet expectations	**Score: 3 Meets expectations**	**Score: 5 Exceeds expectations**
Language Use	Student uses little or no target language and relies heavily on native language word order.	Student uses the target language consistently, but may mix native and target language word order.	Student uses the target language exclusively and integrates target language word order into conversation.
Vocabulary Use	Student uses limited and repetitive language.	Student uses only recently acquired vocabulary.	Student uses both recently and previously acquired vocabulary.

Presentational Task Rubric

	Score: 1 Does not meet expectations	**Score: 3 Meets expectations**	**Score: 5 Exceeds expectations**
Amount of Communication	Student gives limited or no details or examples.	Student gives adequate details or examples.	Student gives consistent details or examples.
Accuracy	Student's accuracy with vocabulary and structures is limited.	Student's accuracy with vocabulary and structures is adequate.	Student's accuracy with vocabulary and structures is exemplary.
Comprehensibility	Student's ideas lack clarity and are difficult to understand.	Student's ideas are adequately clear and fairly well understood.	Student's ideas are precise and easily understood.
Vocabulary Use	Student uses limited and repetitive vocabulary.	Student uses only recently acquired vocabulary.	Student uses both recently and previously acquired vocabulary.

¿Qué está de moda?

1 Si miras la ropa en fotos viejas o en revistas de modas de hace muchos años, ¿qué te parece? ¿Consideras la ropa bonita o fea? Y si miras una revista de modas de hoy, quizás ves ropa muy parecida. Cada año hay nuevos estilos de ropa, pero curiosamente algunos de los estilos de hace unas décadas están de moda hoy. Así que el estilo de la ropa de tus abuelos en los años sesenta ¡puede ser el mismo que tú y tus amigos van a llevar mañana!

2 De los estilos que están aquí, ¿cuáles están de moda en tu escuela ... y cuáles llevas tú?

3 *La ropa negra de los* beatniks

En los años cincuenta, algunos jóvenes son *beatniks*, y llevan sólo ropa negra. Los chicos y las chicas se visten igual, con pantalones, suéteres, botas y chaquetas de cuero. Mucha gente asocia esta ropa con delincuentes juveniles. En realidad, los *beatniks* son artísticos e intelectuales, con inclinación por la poesía, la música y la política.

4 *Las minifaldas y las botas* go-go

A fines de los años sesenta, las minifaldas están de moda. Es un estilo exagerado y muy dramático, pero a las jóvenes ya no les gusta llevar vestidos y faldas hasta la rodilla. Para completar su *look,* las chicas llevan botas *go-go,* que generalmente son blancas. Los colores más populares para la ropa son tonos vivos, fuertes y "psicodélicos" de rosa, verde, anaranjado y morado.

5 *Los vestidos del estilo* granny *y las camisetas* tie-dye

A fines de los años sesenta y a principios de los setenta, muchos jóvenes son *hippies*. Las chicas llevan vestidos largos y flojos con dibujos exóticos de la India, o los vestidos de estilo *granny*, que imitan el estilo de la ropa de las pioneras americanas. Las camisetas *tie-dye* también son muy populares para las chicas y los chicos.

6 *Los zapatos con plataforma*

En los años setenta, los zapatos con plataforma están de moda. Estos zapatos son ideales para las personas bajitas que quieren parecer más altas. ¡Y son perfectas para caminar cuando llueve!

7 *Los jeans*

Antes de los años sesenta, los jeans no se ven mucho en las ciudades. Pero en esa década, muchos estudiantes universitarios empiezan a llevarlos más y más. Los *hippies* llevan los jeans tan a menudo que tienen agujeros. En los años ochenta y noventa, muchos jóvenes compran jeans bastante caros, pero los cortan y les hacen agujeros. Esto es un escándalo para sus padres, que no comprenden por qué sus hijos arruinan su ropa nueva de esta manera. Hoy tantas personas llevan jeans que parecen ser el uniforme más o menos oficial de muchos países.

Practice Test

Answer questions 1–6. Base your answers on the reading *"¿Qué está de moda?"*.

1 Why might the readers wear the same style of clothes as their grandparents?

- **A** It was the most fashionable clothing of the twentieth century.
- **B** Their grandparents were very stylish.
- **C** Styles often repeat themselves.
- **D** They like wearing hand-me-downs.

2 What does the word agujeros mean in paragraph 7?

- **F** pockets
- **G** holes
- **H** buttons
- **J** seams

3 According to the article, why were miniskirts such a dramatic change in women's fashion?

- **A** Skirt lengths previously had been longer.
- **B** They came in psychedelic colors.
- **C** The general public did not approve of them.
- **D** They gave women more freedom of movement.

4 According to this article, what item of clothing has now become the unofficial "uniform" of many people?

- **F** platform shoes
- **G** tie-dyed T-shirts
- **H** blue jeans
- **J** black clothes

5 READ THINK EXPLAIN ¿Qué estilo de ropa de antes no quieres ver nunca más? ¿Por qué no te gusta?

6 READ THINK EXPLAIN Which of the fashions described do you think also made a political or philosophical statement? Explain your answer.

Realidades 2

Nombre ____________ Fecha ____________

Tema 2

Practice Test Answer Sheet

1 Ⓐ Ⓑ Ⓒ Ⓓ   2 Ⓕ Ⓖ Ⓗ Ⓙ   3 Ⓐ Ⓑ Ⓒ Ⓓ

4 Ⓕ Ⓖ Ⓗ Ⓙ

5 READ THINK EXPLAIN

6 READ THINK EXPLAIN

Realidades 2 Nombre ______________ Fecha ______________

Capítulo 3A **Reading Skills: Conexiones, p. 141**

Making and Confirming Inferences

One indication of good readers is their ability to read between the lines of a text. Not only do they literally read and comprehend what a text says, but they also make inferences from what they read. An inference is an educated guess about something written in the text. An inference, because it is a guess, can never be absolutely right or wrong. However, an inference, like a conclusion, can be believable based upon the evidence that is present in the text. Confirming an inference means locating the evidence in the text that leads support to the inference.

Tip

One strategy that can help you as you read poetry and make inferences about what you have read is to write a Question Paper. With a Question Paper, write down the first question that occurs to you as you read a poem. After writing this first question, you have a choice: (1) write another question, or (2) respond to the first question. In responding to a question, you may attempt to answer the question with another question or with a statement that begins with "Maybe."

1. On page 141 in your textbook, read Pablo Neruda's *"Un poema de amor"* in **Actividad 16.** Based on what you have read, fill in the Question Paper below.

Question Paper

Why does the narrator say, "Together we made a turn on the route where love passed"? Does this mean that they ____
____
____.

Was this a good thing or a bad thing for their love? Maybe it was bad because
____.

Or maybe it was good because ____
____.

Is the narrator still together with this woman that he loved? Why or why not?
____
____
____

Sample question:

2. The line *"Juntos hicimos un recodo en la ruta donde el amor pasó"* would seem to suggest that

- **A** it was not the narrator alone who decided for the lovers to make a turn in their relationship.
- **B** it was the narrator's decision to make a turn in the relationship.
- **C** there was never any love in this relationship.
- **D** too much travel and long periods apart from each other can destroy a relationship.

 Reading Skills: Lectura pp. 146–147

Determining the Main Idea and Identifying Relevant Details

To know the relevant details in a reading passage is to know which ones are most important. The first step in identifying the relevant details is to identify the main idea of the passage. The relevant details are the ones that help support the main idea. After reading a passage, good readers ask themselves, "What is this passage mostly about?" and "Which details in the passage help support, explain, or prove the main idea?"

Tip

Some readers are better able to identify the main idea and the relevant details when they have a graphic organizer. The graphic organizer below presents the main idea as if it were the roof of a house and the relevant details as the columns supporting the roof or main idea.

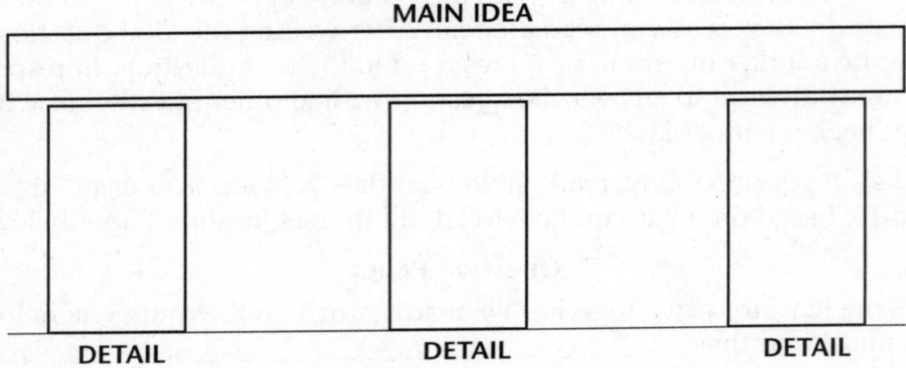

1. On pages 146–147 in your textbook, re-read the **Lectura,** ***La unidad en la comunidad internacional.*** After reading, write the statements below in the graphic organizer. One statement is irrelevant.
   - In educational exchanges, young people from the United States learn about the culture of the country of their sister city by living with families in the sister city.
   - Selling the products of one sister city in the stores of the other sister city is one way to establish economic exchanges.
   - The International Sister Cities program promotes understanding between residents of different countries through economic, cultural, and educational exchanges.
   - The Sister Cities program was created in 1956 by President Dwight D. Eisenhower.

Sample question:

2. Which statement below does NOT help support the main idea of the **Lectura,** ***La unidad en la comunidad internacional***?

   A Selling the products of one sister city in the stores of the other sister city is one way to establish economic exchanges.
   B In educational exchanges, young people from the United States learn about the culture of the country of their sister city by living with families in the sister city.
   C The Sister Cities program was created in 1956 by President Dwight D. Eisenhower.
   D Cultural exchanges could include hosting a dance and food festival in honor of one's sister city.

Integrated Performance Assessment
Unit theme: ¿Qué hiciste ayer?

Context for the Integrated Performance Assessment: You and a group of students from your school are in Mexico for the summer living and studying at an international school. You are having a wonderful time, but you miss your own family. You decide to call them and tell them what you have been doing.

Interpretive Task: Watch the *Videohistoria: ¿Qué hiciste esta mañana?* from *Realidades 2, DVD 2, Capítulo 3A.* Listen as the students talk about what they did earlier today and write down 3 things they did. Think about what you did yesterday in Mexico and write down 3 things you did.

Interpersonal Task: Tell one of your classmates at the international school what you did yesterday. Ask him/ her about what he/she did yesterday. Continue talking about what both of you did yesterday until you have discussed 5 or 6 different activities. Tell each other whether the activities were fun, interesting, or boring.

Presentational Task: You call home, but no one is there. Leave a message on the answering machine greeting your family, telling them you're having fun, and telling them what you did yesterday.

Interpersonal Task Rubric

	Score: 1 Does not meet expectations	Score: 3 Meets expectations	Score: 5 Exceeds expectations
Language Use	Student uses little or no target language and relies heavily on native language word order.	Student uses the target language consistently, but may mix native and target language word order.	Student uses the target language exclusively and integrates target language word order into conversation.
Vocabulary Use	Student uses limited and repetitive language.	Student uses only recently acquired vocabulary.	Student uses both recently and previously acquired vocabulary.

Presentational Task Rubric

	Score: 1 Does not meet expectations	Score: 3 Meets expectations	Score: 5 Exceeds expectations
Amount of Communication	Student gives limited or no details or examples.	Student gives adequate details or examples.	Student gives consistent details or examples.
Accuracy	Student's accuracy with vocabulary and structures is limited.	Student's accuracy with vocabulary and structures is adequate.	Student's accuracy with vocabulary and structures is exemplary.
Comprehensibility	Student's ideas lack clarity and are difficult to understand.	Student's ideas are adequately clear and fairly well understood.	Student's ideas are precise and easily understood.
Vocabulary Use	Student uses limited and repetitive vocabulary.	Student uses only recently acquired vocabulary.	Student uses both recently and previously acquired vocabulary.

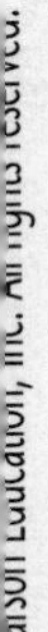

Realidades 2 Nombre ______________________ Fecha ______________

Capítulo 3B **Reading Skills: Fondo cultural, p. 172**

Recognizing the Use of Comparison and Contrast

To recognize comparison and contrast in a reading passage, good readers can point out how items or ideas in the reading passage are similar to or different from each other. Sometimes writers will directly state that they are comparing or contrasting items in a reading passage. Other times readers might recognize items in a reading passage that could be compared or contrasted even though the writer might not have presented the information for that purpose.

Tip

With comparison and contrast, one of the biggest challenges for students is to recognize the need to narrow the focus of your comparisons and contrasts. When producing a comparison-contrast chart, some students will state things that are obvious. For example, you might choose to compare and contrast apples and oranges and then focus only on the color and shape of the fruits. Then you state the obvious: *One is red while the other is orange; both are sort of round in shape*. Professional writers, on the other hand, are less likely to state the obvious. Instead, they aim to teach readers something that readers likely do not already know.

1. On page 172 in your textbook, re-read the **Fondo cultural,** ***"Permiso de manejar."*** After you have finished reading, determine which missing places in the chart can be filled with information from the reading passage. Fill in only those blanks.

Three Ways to Compare/ Contrast Driving Requirements	*All Spanish-speaking Countries*	*Spain*	*Argentina*	*United States*
A	Identity documents and medical records			
B				
C Age required for different driving privileges				

Sample question:

2. Based on the information presented in the **Fondo cultural,** ***"Permiso de manejar."*** which statement below is true?

A It is easier to get a driver's license in Spain than it is in the United States.
B You must be in good physical and mental health to get a driver's license in Spanish-speaking countries.
C You can drive a moped at a younger age in Argentina than in Spain.
D Passing a driving exam is a requirement for a license in Argentina but not in Spain.

Reading Skills: Lectura, pp. 174–175

Drawing Conclusions

To draw a conclusion is to form an opinion based on evidence. Sometimes the evidence presented to readers is very limited, but they must ensure that their evidence-based opinions make sense.

Conclusion statements are rarely right or wrong. They are often presented as believable or not. If you are successful at drawing conclusions from your reading, then you likely are skilled at finding evidence in your reading that supports your conclusions.

Conclusions are only as strong as the evidence on which they are based. Conclusions based on little evidence are not as believable as conclusions based on a lot of different kinds of evidence. You must also be willing to change your conclusions as more evidence becomes available in the reading passage.

Tip

One strategy that helps students as they draw conclusions is to use "If-Then" statements with their evidence and conclusions. If a conclusion does not make sense, then it will become obvious when presented in an "If-Then" statement. Also, as more evidence is presented in the "If" statements, the conclusions in the "Then" statements will likely change.

1. On pages 174–175 in your textbook re-read the **Lectura,** ***Guía del buen conductor.*** Then complete the sentences that follow. Can you draw more than one possible conclusion for the evidence presented below?

   A **If** you should reduce your speed when a highway is not lighted,
   and

   B **if** you should reduce your speed when it is raining,
   then one could conclude that

   ____.

   Now add this third piece of evidence:

   C **If** you should drive 50% slower at night than during the day,
   then based on points A, B, and C, one could conclude that

   ____.

Sample question:

2. Based on the information presented in the **Lectura,** ***Guía del buen conductor,*** one could conclude that
   - **A** good drivers are more likely to avoid driving at night.
   - **B** many accidents occur even when the drivers are paying attention to the highway.
   - **C** good drivers are not affected by the conditions of the driving surface.
   - **D** controlling driving speed is one effective way to avoid driving accidents.

Capítulo 3B

Integrated Performance Assessment

Unit theme: ¿Cómo se va ... ?

Context for the Integrated Performance Assessment: Recently there have been a number of automobile accidents involving teenagers in your community. As a result, your parents have decided that you cannot get your driver's license until you are 18 years old. You are not happy about their decision and want to change their mind!

Interpretive Task: Read the *Lectura: Guía del buen conductor* on pages 174-175 of *Realidades 2*. Find strategies that can help you be a good driver. Make a list of at least 5 strategies.

Interpersonal Task: Read the list of strategies to your partner and listen to your partner's list. Discuss other strategies from the *Lectura*. Decide on the 6 best strategies that might help you convince your parents.

Presentational Task: Make the presentation that you hope will convince your parents to let you get your driver's license to a group of students in your Spanish class so that they can give you feedback on your presentation's effectiveness. Don't forget to mention the 6 strategies that you and your partner discussed.

Interpersonal Task Rubric

	Score: 1 Does not meet expectations	**Score: 3 Meets expectations**	**Score: 5 Exceeds expectations**
Language Use	Student uses little or no target language and relies heavily on native language word order.	Student uses the target language consistently, but may mix native and target language word order.	Student uses the target language exclusively and integrates target language word order into conversation.
Vocabulary Use	Student uses limited and repetitive language.	Student uses only recently acquired vocabulary.	Student uses both recently and previously acquired vocabulary.

Presentational Task Rubric

	Score: 1 Does not meet expectations	**Score: 3 Meets expectations**	**Score: 5 Exceeds expectations**
Amount of Communication	Student gives limited or no details or examples.	Student gives adequate details or examples.	Student gives consistent details or examples.
Accuracy	Student's accuracy with vocabulary and structures is limited.	Student's accuracy with vocabulary and structures is adequate.	Student's accuracy with vocabulary and structures is exemplary.
Comprehensibility	Student's ideas lack clarity and are difficult to understand.	Student's ideas are adequately clear and fairly well understood.	Student's ideas are precise and easily understood.
Vocabulary Use	Student uses limited and repetitive vocabulary.	Student uses only recently acquired vocabulary.	Student uses both recently and previously acquired vocabulary.

La Casa de los Azulejos

1 En Nueva España, que es como se llama México hace muchos años, vive un joven muy rico. Este joven, que se llama Luis, siempre tiene conflictos con su padre porque le encanta gastar su dinero en lujos extravagantes.

2 —¡Con muchos sacrificios gané nuestra fortuna, y ahora tú vas a terminar con ella! —le dice su padre a Luis.— Por favor, hijo, ¡piensa en lo que haces!— Pero Luis sólo piensa en gastar dinero y llamar la atención de todos con sus lujos.

3 La fama de Luis y cómo gasta la fortuna de su padre llegó a los oídos del virrey (el representante del rey español en Nueva España). El virrey dice con mucho sarcasmo: "Ése no hará nunca casa de azulejos." Este comentario quiere decir que Luis nunca va a hacer nada bueno con su dinero. Para recuperar su honor, Luis compró una hermosa mansión en el centro de la ciudad y la decoró con brillantes azulejos. Estos azulejos tienen bellos dibujos en azul, blanco y amarillo. Así, dice la tradición popular, es cómo originó la Casa de los Azulejos.

4 Se dice también que unos años después, Luis compró muebles elegantes para la casa y organizó una fiesta con baile en honor de sus padres. Durante la fiesta Luis notó que un reloj muy caro desapareció de su lugar. Entonces los músicos ya no tocaron y Luis dijo a los invitados:

5 —Alguien me robó un reloj de oro y diamantes que me regaló el rey. Miren, el reloj ya no está allí, al lado de la ventana. Pero no importa porque a las doce de la noche, el reloj va a tocar música que todos ustedes van a oír en la sala. Así vamos a saber quién es el ladrón.

6 Para darle al ladrón la oportunidad de devolver el reloj, la sala se quedó sin luz.

7 Cuando volvieron a poner las luces, todos vieron el reloj otra vez en su lugar. Entonces la fiesta continuó.

8 ¡Ninguno de los invitados sabe que el reloj de Luis no toca música! Todo fue una ingeniosa idea de Luis para recuperar su reloj.

Practice Test

Answer questions 1–6. Base your answers on the reading *"La casa de los Azulejos."*

1 Where does this story take place?

- **A** in Spain
- **B** in New Mexico
- **C** in Mexico
- **D** in Azulejos

2 Why was Luis's father so unhappy with him?

- **F** Luis was wasting the family fortune.
- **G** Luis was always breaking the law.
- **H** Luis was more famous than he was.
- **J** Luis never bought anything for his father.

3 How did Luis react to the viceroy's negative comment about him?

- **A** He laughed about it.
- **B** He became angry and confronted him about it.
- **C** He decided to try to rebuild his reputation.
- **D** He paid no attention to it.

4 What is the origin of the Casa de los Azulejos?

- **F** It's the mansion that the king gave Luis.
- **G** It's the mansion that Luis bought and decorated with blue, white, and yellow tiles.
- **H** It's the mansion that Luis bought from his father.
- **J** It's the mansion that Luis's father bought.

5 Why did Luis say that the clock was going to play music at midnight?

- **A** to impress his guests
- **B** to know the time
- **C** to catch the thief
- **D** to play a joke

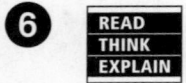

6 READ THINK EXPLAIN ¿Por qué crees que el dinero es la causa de muchos conflictos entre padres e hijos? ¿Cómo reaccionan tus padres cuando no piensas antes de gastar dinero?

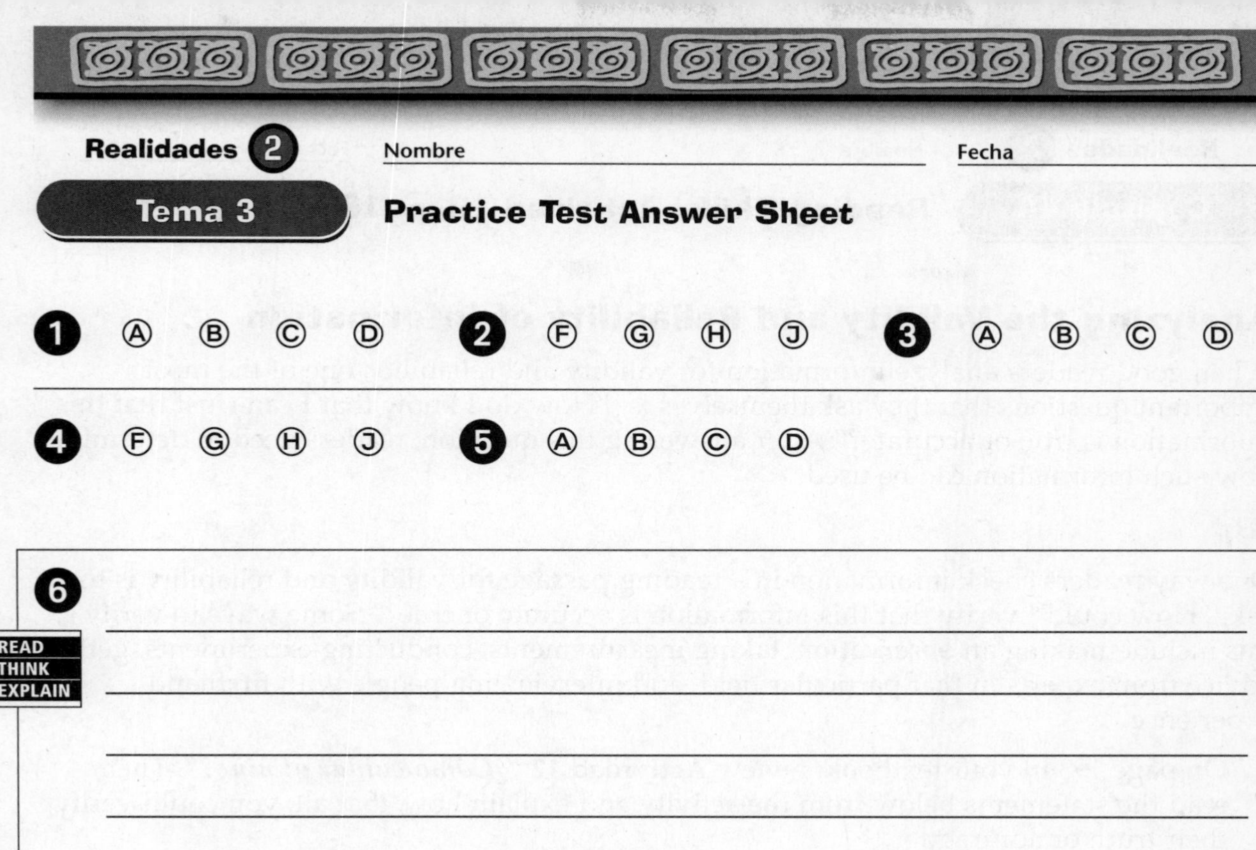

Realidades 2 | Nombre | Fecha

Tema 3

Practice Test Answer Sheet

1 Ⓐ Ⓑ Ⓒ Ⓓ   2 Ⓕ Ⓖ Ⓗ Ⓙ   3 Ⓐ Ⓑ Ⓒ Ⓓ

4 Ⓕ Ⓖ Ⓗ Ⓙ   5 Ⓐ Ⓑ Ⓒ Ⓓ

6

READ THINK EXPLAIN

Analyzing the Validity and Reliability of Information

When good readers analyze information for validity and reliability, one of the most important questions that they ask themselves is, "How do I know that I can trust that this information is true or accurate?" After answering this question, readers need to determine how such information can be used.

Tip

One way readers check information in a reading passage for validity and reliability is to ask, "How could I verify that this information is accurate or true?" Some ways to verify this include making an observation, taking measurements, conducting experiments, getting advice from experts in that particular field, and interviewing people with firsthand experience.

1. On page 193 in your textbook, review **Actividad 12 *"¿Cómo cuidar al niño?"***. Then, read the statements below from the activity and explain how, if at all, you could verify their truth or accuracy.
   - *Nuestros maestros tienen preparación professional.*
   - *Nuestros maestros comprenden las necesidades del niño según su edad.*
   - *Tenemos ya 25 años de experiencia.*
   - *Cuidar a sus niños es nuestra pasión.*
   - *Trabajamos todos los días para desarrollar en sus niños la capacidad de desarrollar hábitos higiénicos y cuidados personales.*

Sample question:

2. If a family that was interested in sending their child to *Guardería infantil Rincón del niño* hired you to verify the accuracy of the information in their advertisement, which detail would likely be HARDEST to verify?
   A Taking care of your children is our passion.
   B We already have 25 years of experience.
   C Our teachers understand the age-appropriate needs of your child.
   D Our teachers have professional training.

Analyzing the Effectiveness of Complex Elements of Plot

When reading stories, it is important for readers to identify the protagonist, or main character, of the story. The protagonist usually has a goal, and it is the protagonist's attempt to reach that goal that moves the plot of the story. The plot can be summed up as all the actions that occur as the protagonist attempts to reach his or her goal. While attempting to reach his or her goal, the protagonist encounters problems or conflicts that must be resolved. The climax of the story is the point when it becomes clear that the protagonist will or will not reach his or her goal. Good readers can explain how various elements of the plot, such as the protagonist's goals or conflicts, affect the outcome of the story.

Tip

1. One way that readers can identify and understand various plot elements is to use a chart. After reviewing the **Lectura,** ***El grillo y el jaguar*** on pages 202 and 203 in your textbook, fill in the information required in the chart below. It is possible that in a simple fable such as ***"El grillo y el jaguar,"*** the protagonist might encounter only one conflict and the resolution of this one conflict might be the climax of the story. In more complex stories, the protagonist would likely encounter a series of conflicts before the story reaches its climax.

Who is the protagonist?

____

What is his/her goal?

____

What conflicts does he/she encounter?

____

What is the outcome of each conflict?

____

When is the climax of the story?

____

Sample question:

2. What is the best description of the cricket's conflict?
   - **A** The cricket likes to sing all the time, but the other animals of the jungle don't like the singing.
   - **B** The cricket would like to beat the jaguar in a race, but the jaguar is much faster than the cricket.
   - **C** The cricket is hungry, but cannot eat unless the jaguar brings him food.
   - **D** The cricket wins the race with the jaguar, but the jaguar refuses to give the cricket a prize

Realidades 2

Capítulo 4A

Integrated Performance Assessment
Unit theme: Cuando éramos niños

Context for the Integrated Performance Assessment: The Spanish Club at your school is very proud of the Web site it maintains. Students from many Spanish-speaking countries have enjoyed learning about the members of the club and its activities. The club has decided to post a new link called *"Cuando éramos niños"* where each member will post a photo of himself/herself as a child along with a description of what he/she was like as a child.

Interpretive Task: Watch the *Videohistoria: ¿Cómo era de niña?* from *Realidades 2, DVD 2, Capítulo 4A.* Listen carefully as the students discuss their childhood. When you hear something that reminds you of your childhood, write it down. Afterwards, write a few sentences that describe what you were like as a child and some activities you used to do as a child.

Interpersonal Task: Discuss your childhood with a friend in Spanish class. Ask each other questions in order to learn more about what your friend was like and the activities he/she used to do.

Presentational Task: Write a description of yourself as a child. Say what you were like and the activities that you used to do. Be sure to attach a cute photo or drawing of yourself for the Web site!

Interpersonal Task Rubric

	Score: 1 Does not meet expectations	Score: 3 Meets expectations	Score: 5 Exceeds expectations
Language Use	Student uses little or no target language and relies heavily on native language word order.	Student uses the target language consistently, but may mix native and target language word order.	Student uses the target language exclusively and integrates target language word order into conversation.
Vocabulary Use	Student uses limited and repetitive language.	Student uses only recently acquired vocabulary.	Student uses both recently and previously acquired vocabulary.

Presentational Task Rubric

	Score: 1 Does not meet expectations	Score: 3 Meets expectations	Score: 5 Exceeds expectations
Amount of Communication	Student gives limited or no details or examples.	Student gives adequate details or examples.	Student gives consistent details or examples.
Accuracy	Student's accuracy with vocabulary and structures is limited.	Student's accuracy with vocabulary and structures is adequate.	Student's accuracy with vocabulary and structures is exemplary.
Comprehensibility	Student's ideas lack clarity and are difficult to understand.	Student's ideas are adequately clear and fairly well understood.	Student's ideas are precise and easily understood.
Vocabulary Use	Student uses limited and repetitive vocabulary.	Student uses only recently acquired vocabulary.	Student uses both recently and previously acquired vocabulary.

Reading Skills: Conexiones, p. 223

Locates, Gathers, Analyzes, and Evaluates Written Information

By showing that they can locate, gather, analyze, and evaluate information from one or more reading passages, good readers demonstrate that they know how to conduct research. On a test, readers are often asked to locate, gather, analyze, and evaluate information from a reading passage and then show how to put that information to good use.

Tip

Readers who conduct research are skilled at translating information from their reading into their own words. If you encounter information in one format such as in a paragraph or in a chart, you should be able to restate that information in a different format such as in a list or as bullets. This is how you demonstrate your comprehension of what you have read.

1. On page 223 in your textbook review the **Conexiones** in **Actividad 16** ***"El Día de la Independencia."*** Then use information from the reading to fill in the blanks on the chart below.

Liberated Country	Liberated From	Date	What Influenced the Country's Liberation?
U.S.A.	________	________	________
France	________	________	________
Spain	________	________	________
Mexico	________	________	________
Colombia	________	________	________
Venezuela	________	________	________
Perú	________	________	________
Ecuador	________	________	________
Bolivia	________	________	________

Sample question:

2. Imagine that you need to write a report for your history class about how as time passes, countries change their positions in the world, sometimes even assuming opposing roles. Which information from the chart above could illustrate this point?
   - **A** The American and French independence movements were great examples for the countries of Latin America.
   - **B** The French people gained independence from the French monarchy.
   - **C** Miguel Hidalgo began the Mexican War for Independence around the same time that Simón Bolívar led the Colombian movement for independence.
   - **D** Not long after the Spanish fought for their independence from the French, Simón Bolívar was leading the people of Colombia, Venezuela, Perú, Ecuador, and Bolivia in wars of independence against the Spanish.

Identifying Methods of Development and Patterns of Organization

Good readers understand the tools and techniques of authors. To identify the methods of development used by an author in a text, you must first determine the author's purpose by asking, "Why was this text written?" After determining the author's purpose, you next ask, "What techniques did the author use to achieve his or her purpose?" These techniques are known as methods of development and could include, among other things, the organization pattern, the word choice, or the sentence structure used in the text.

Tip

One common purpose for writing is to make a request. The request usually takes the form of a letter. Effective writers will begin by convincing the reader that they are people whose requests should be taken seriously. You might do this by showing that you are successful, trustworthy, honest, or caring. Once you establish that you are a person whose requests are worthy of consideration, you then present your requests. The letter of request often concludes by mentioning something nice and thanking the reader for his or her attention.

1. On pages 228 and 229 in your textbook, review the **Lectura, *El seis de enero*.** Pay particular attention to the two letters written to the *Reyes Magos*. Then, answer the questions that follow.

   A How does Carolina convince the *Reyes Magos* that she is a person whose requests are worthy of consideration?

   ____

   ____

   B What does Carolina request?

   ____

   ____

   C How does Carolina conclude her letter?

   ____

   ____

Sample question:

2. In the letter written to the *Reyes Magos* by José Alejandro and Jorge Andrés, which is NOT a way that the writers show themselves to be people whose requests are worthy of consideration?
   A They say that they behave well.
   B They say that they get good grades in school.
   C They say that they do all their homework.
   D They say that they are kind to the poor children.

Realidades 2
Capítulo 4B

Integrated Performance Assessment
Unit theme: Celebrando los días festivos

Context for the Integrated Performance Task: A group of students from Spain is spending 3 weeks at your school. Because family celebrations are important events in Spain, the students would like to learn about family celebrations in the United States. Your class has been asked to talk about holidays or celebrations that were important to you during your childhood.

Interpretive Task: Watch the *Videohistoria: La fiesta de San Pedro* from *Realidades 2, DVD 2, Capítulo 4B.* Listen as Igancio describes the customs and activities of *La fiesta de San Pedro.* Think about a holiday or family celebration that was important to you during your childhood. Why was it important to you? Write a few sentences about how you and your family used to celebrate the event.

Interpersonal Task: Tell your partner the event that you have chosen and why it was important to you. Describe how you used to celebrate it with your family. Listen to your partner's description. Ask each other questions about aspects of the celebration that your partner did not mention. You might ask about music, food, special clothing, and other customs and activities.

Presentational Task: Make an oral presentation to the students from Spain telling them all about the holiday or family celebration that was important to you during your childhood, why it was important, and how you used to celebrate it with your family.

Interpersonal Task Rubric

	Score: 1 Does not meet expectations	Score: 3 Meets expectations	Score: 5 Exceeds expectations
Language Use	Student uses little or no target language and relies heavily on native language word order.	Student uses the target language consistently, but may mix native and target language word order.	Student uses the target language exclusively and integrates target language word order into conversation.
Vocabulary Use	Student uses limited and repetitive language.	Student uses only recently acquired vocabulary.	Student uses both recently and previously acquired vocabulary.

Presentational Task Rubric

	Score: 1 Does not meet expectations	Score: 3 Meets expectations	Score: 5 Exceeds expectations
Amount of Communication	Student gives limited or no details or examples.	Student gives adequate details or examples.	Student gives consistent details or examples.
Accuracy	Student's accuracy with vocabulary and structures is limited.	Student's accuracy with vocabulary and structures is adequate.	Student's accuracy with vocabulary and structures is exemplary.
Comprehensibility	Student's ideas lack clarity and are difficult to understand.	Student's ideas are adequately clear and fairly well understood.	Student's ideas are precise and easily understood.
Vocabulary Use	Student uses limited and repetitive vocabulary.	Student uses only recently acquired vocabulary.	Student uses both recently and previously acquired vocabulary.

El parque

Adaptado de un poema de Elizabeth Millán

1 De niño Manolito jugaba en este parque.
Allí está el árbol que le gustaba trepar.
Aquí había una cuerda que le gustaba saltar.
Y el patio de recreo por donde montaba
en su triciclo
es hoy un feo y aburrido
centro comercial.

2 De joven llegaba al parque también Manolo
con sus amigos de la escuela.
Eran chicos bien educados y obedientes,
(bueno, ¡casi siempre!)
Manolo era generoso y compartía
con ellos todo lo que tenía:
sus colecciones de muñecos, tarjetas, monedas y sellos
y también ideas, sueños y penas.

3 Hace poco que Manuel
y otros universitarios,
se quedaban hasta muy tarde
hablando de todo:
de su presente, de su futuro,
de la política y del mundo
(y de las novias y del fútbol).

4 Don Manuel llegaba después,
tan serio con su periódico,
de lunes a viernes
en camino al trabajo.
Los domingos pasaba
con su mujer y sus tres hijos,
después de tomar paella
en Casa Paco
y antes de su siesta.

5 Y hoy sólo este viejecito siempre pasa
y se queda sólo un momento.
Busca el árbol que trepaba,
el patio de recreo donde jugaba,
y el lugar por donde
caminaba con su mujer
y sus hijos.
Y llora porque está solo y
sólo los ve en sus recuerdos.

6 Y se va lentamente,
muy lentamente ...

Practice Test

Answer questions 1–6. Base your answers on the reading, *"El parque."*

1 According to the poem, don Manuel

- **A** never thinks about his childhood.
- **B** thinks about his past.
- **C** often talks about his work.
- **D** still likes politics and soccer.

2 Why does the writer use the names Manolito, Manolo, and don Manuel?

- **F** They are the grandson, son, and father of the writer.
- **G** They are three different people.
- **H** They are the names the same man had at different ages of his life.
- **J** They are variants of the same name.

3 At the end of the poem, the reader realizes that

- **A** this is just a dream.
- **B** don Manuel doesn't like to take walks in the park.
- **C** don Manuel lives in the park.
- **D** don Manuel is now old and lonely.

4 Using context clues, what is the meaning of the word *trepar* in verse 1?

- **F** to collect
- **G** to climb
- **H** to plant
- **J** to ride

5 READ THINK EXPLAIN — What are your most vivid memories of your early childhood? Describe them in a short paragraph.

6 

Imagina que tienes ochenta años. ¿Cuáles son tus recuerdos? Escribe un párrafo describiendo tu vida de niño (niña), de joven y de adulto (adulta). Describe a tus amigos, a tu familia, tus actividades favoritas y tus temas favoritos de conversación.

Realidades 2 Nombre Fecha

Tema 4

Practice Test Answer Sheet

1 Ⓐ Ⓑ Ⓒ Ⓓ 2 Ⓕ Ⓖ Ⓗ Ⓙ 3 Ⓐ Ⓑ Ⓒ Ⓓ

4 Ⓕ Ⓖ Ⓗ Ⓙ

5 READ THINK EXPLAIN

6 READ THINK CREATE

Reading Skills: Actividad 20, p. 253

Recognizing Cause-Effect Relationships

To recognize cause-effect relationships in fiction, nonfiction, drama, or poetry, readers should be aware of why things happen (causes) as well as the consequences or results of actions (effects) in a reading passage.

Tip

Readers who read with a purpose are more likely to comprehend what they have read than those that read passively. To read with a purpose, you should have a question in your mind as you read. Your reading then becomes an active search for the answer to your question.

One way to develop into someone who reads with a purpose is to pause periodically in your reading and ask "Why?" Good readers formulate questions that begin with "Why?" whose answers can be located in the text. This is also an effective way to recognize cause-effect relationships in a text.

1. On page 253 in your textbook, review **Actividad 20** ***"En caso de un incendio..."*** After you have finished reading, answer the first two questions below. Then formulate your own "Why" questions and answers based on what you have read.

   Why should hotel guests know where to find all the exits in a hotel?

   ____

   ____

   Why should hotel guests touch their hotel door when responding to a fire alarm in a hotel?

   ____

   ____

   Why ____?

   ____

   ____

   Why ____?

   ____

   ____

Sample question:

2. Based on your reading of ***"Cómo sobrevivir un incendio en el hotel,"*** why do people panic in a hotel fire?
   - **A** Because their hotel doors are often too hot to open.
   - **B** Because they cannot use the elevator in a fire.
   - **C** Because they usually do not know what to do during a hotel fire.
   - **D** Because there are often not enough exits for the hotel guests to use when fleeing a fire.

Reading Skills: Lectura, pp. 256–257

Synthesizing Information from Multiple Sources to Draw Conclusions

Often readers are asked to look at two or more reading passages and make connections between the different passages. When readers synthesize information, they are forming new ideas based on what they have read in the different reading passages.

Tip

When synthesizing information from various sources, readers benefit when they take notes. While you read, you might underline or highlight information that you find to be particularly important. After you read, you might write out a list of the most important items from the passage.

1. On pages 256 and 257 of your textbook, review the **Lectura** and then list what you believe to be the most important information in the passages below.

Desastre en Valdivia

a ______

b ______

c ______

d ______

La escala Richter

a ______

b ______

c ______

d ______

El tsunami

a ______

b ______

c ______

d ______

¿Qué debes hacer...?

a ______

b ______

c ______

d ______

Sample question:

2. Based on all the reading passages in the **Lectura**, what would be true if the earthquake that hit Valdivia in 1960 was a 3.0 on the Richter scale?
   A It might not have been felt by the residents of Valdivia.
   B A tsunami would have hit Valdivia 10–20 minutes after the earthquake.
   C Two million people would have lost their homes.
   D Residents would have stayed away from glass windows, pictures, and fireplaces.

Realidades 2

Capítulo 5A

Integrated Performance Assessment

Unit theme: Un acto heroico

Context for the Integrated Performance Assessment: A group of students from Guatemala is coming to spend several weeks with you and your classmates. Some of the students are nervous and want to know if there have been natural disasters in your community. They also want to know if there are emergency and rescue services in your community.

Interpretive Task: Listen to several reporters describe disasters in their community on *Realidades 2, Audio Program DVD: Cap. 5A, Track 8.* (Don't worry about the directions given on the DVD itself. Use these directions instead.) Write down the disaster that each reporter is describing. Afterwards, draw a circle around each disaster that can happen in your community.

Interpersonal Task: Compare your circled items with a friend in Spanish class. Brainstorm other disasters that could occur or could not occur in your community, and add them to you list. If you can think of a specific disaster that occurred, write down information about it. Discuss the emergency and rescue services in your community. What services are there? How do they help? Should the students be nervous about coming to your community?

Presentational Task: Write an e-mail to one of the students from Guatemala telling him/her not to worry about coming to your community. Include specific and detailed information about the kinds of disasters that do and do not occur in your community. Describe the emergency and rescue services available and explain what they do to help.

Interpersonal Task Rubric

	Score: 1 Does not meet expectations	Score: 3 Meets expectations	Score: 5 Exceeds expectations
Language Use	Student uses little or no target language and relies heavily on native language word order.	Student uses the target language consistently, but may mix native and target language word order.	Student uses the target language exclusively and integrates target language word order into conversation.
Vocabulary Use	Student uses limited and repetitive language.	Student uses only recently acquired vocabulary.	Student uses both recently and previously acquired vocabulary.

Presentational Task Rubric

	Score: 1 Does not meet expectations	Score: 3 Meets expectations	Score: 5 Exceeds expectations
Amount of Communication	Student gives limited or no details or examples.	Student gives adequate details or examples.	Student gives consistent details or examples.
Accuracy	Student's accuracy with vocabulary and structures is limited.	Student's accuracy with vocabulary and structures is adequate.	Student's accuracy with vocabulary and structures is exemplary.
Comprehensibility	Student's ideas lack clarity and are difficult to understand.	Student's ideas are adequately clear and fairly well understood.	Student's ideas are precise and easily understood.
Vocabulary Use	Student uses limited and repetitive vocabulary.	Student uses only recently acquired vocabulary.	Student uses both recently and previously acquired vocabulary.

Reading Skills: Conexiones, p. 279

Recognizing the Use of Comparison and Contrast

To recognize comparison and contrast in a reading passage, good readers can point out how items or ideas in the reading passage are similar to or different from each other. Sometimes writers will directly state that they are comparing or contrasting items in a reading passage. Other times readers might recognize items in a reading passage that could be compared or contrasted even though the writer might not have presented the information for that purpose.

Tip

Writers tend to use common organization patterns or formats when comparing and contrasting. If A and B represent different items to be compared and contrasted, one organization pattern would be to describe item A in detail and then in a separate paragraph to describe item B. In another organization pattern, the writer might use one paragraph to show how A and B are similar and then use a separate paragraph to show how A and B are different. You should be able to comprehend compare-contrast information in one format and be able to restate the information in another format.

1. On page 279 in your textbook, re-read **Actividad 21, *"Los dos tipos de lesiones deportivas."*** After you have finished reading, fill in the comparison-contrast essay below.

   Acute traumatic injuries and chronic injuries are similar in some ways. First, they both can be the result of participating in ____________. Furthermore, the actual damage to the athlete's body can be the same. For example, both ____________ and tearing of a ____________ could be the result of an acute traumatic injury or of a chronic injury. Finally, one part of the body, the ____________, seems susceptible to both kinds of injuries.

   In spite of their similarities, acute traumatic injuries and chronic injuries also differ in some ways. First, they differ in their causes. While acute traumatic injuries are caused by ____________, chronic injuries are more likely to result from ____________. Secondly, while both kinds of injuries could lead to broken bones, a broken bone from an acute traumatic injury is likely to be the result of ____________ while the broken bone from a chronic injury is likely to have been caused by ____________.

Sample question:

2. How does the cause of acute traumatic injury differ from the cause of chronic injury?
   - A Acute traumatic injuries are more likely to affect the ankles and wrists while chronic injuries are more likely to affect the shoulders and the elbows.
   - B Acute traumatic injuries are more likely to result from an intense blow while chronic injuries are caused by continuous and excessive use.
   - C Both acute traumatic injuries and chronic injuries could lead to broken bones or torn tendons.
   - D Acute traumatic injuries could include stretched or torn muscles while chronic injuries could include bursitis.

Realidades 2 | Nombre ______ | Fecha ______

Capítulo 5B **Reading Skills: Lectura, pp. 282–283**

Identifying Methods of Development and Patterns of Organization

Good readers understand the tools and techniques of authors. To identify the methods of development used by an author in a text, you must first determine the author's purpose by asking, "Why was this text written?" After determining the author's purpose, you next ask, "What techniques did the author use to achieve his or her purpose?" These techniques are known as methods of development and could include the organization pattern, the word choice, or the sentence structure used in the text.

Tip

One common form of communication is the public service announcement (PSA) to promote a charitable or non-profit organization. PSA's rarely rely on factual information alone to communicate their message. They often rely on emotional appeals to gain the public's interest in the mission of the charitable or non-profit organization. While factual information might appeal to the public's intellect and its desire to know things, emotional appeals target the feelings of the public and often encourage the public to take action.

1. On pages 282 and 283 in your textbook, review the **Lectura, *Mejorar la salud para todos*** and pay particular attention to the sections that feature celebrities. Then complete the chart below.

	Summary of the Celebrity's Message	How Does the Message Make You Feel?
Luis Enrique		
Don Francisco		
Mercedes Sosa		

Sample question:

2. Which celebrity's emotional appeal might cause the public to react with a sense of shame or guilt?

A When Luis Enrique says that life puts us to the test.
B When Luis Enrique tells people to say "no" to drugs and "yes" to life.
C When Don Francisco says that donating blood is the greatest gift.
D When Mercedes Sosa tells people not to fail their children—to get those children vaccinated.

Realidades 2

Capítulo 5B

Integrated Performance Assessment
Unit theme: Un accidente

Context for the Integrated Performance Assessment: Next month is "Accident Prevention Month" in your community. The local fire department wants to publish a brochure in Spanish on how to avoid accidents at home and in the neighborhood. They want to include descriptions of personal accidents in the brochure hoping that these descriptions will help others avoid similar accidents. The fire department has asked your class to help by submitting descriptions of accidents that have happened to you.

Interpretive Task: Watch the *Videohistoria: ¡El pobrecito soy yo!* from *Realidades 2, DVD 3, Capítulo 5B* and listen as Raúl describes an accident that happened to him. What was he doing when the accident happened? How did it happen? Was he injured? What happened to him afterwards? Now think about an accident that happened to you and write a brief description in Spanish of what happened. Include the same kind of details that Raúl gave.

Interpersonal Task: Describe your accident to a group of 2 or 3 students in your class. Listen as they describe their accidents. Discuss advice you want to suggest to others so that they don't have the same kind of accident.

Presentational Task: Write a description of your accident and send it to the fire department so that they can include it in their brochure. Be sure to include the advice you have for others so that they won't have the same kind of accident.

Interpersonal Task Rubric

	Score: 1 Does not meet expectations	Score: 3 Meets expectations	Score: 5 Exceeds expectations
Language Use	Student uses little or no target language and relies heavily on native language word order.	Student uses the target language consistently, but may mix native and target language word order.	Student uses the target language exclusively and integrates target language word order into conversation.
Vocabulary Use	Student uses limited and repetitive language.	Student uses only recently acquired vocabulary.	Student uses both recently and previously acquired vocabulary.

Presentational Task Rubric

	Score: 1 Does not meet expectations	Score: 3 Meets expectations	Score: 5 Exceeds expectations
Amount of Communication	Student gives limited or no details or examples.	Student gives adequate details or examples.	Student gives consistent details or examples.
Accuracy	Student's accuracy with vocabulary and structures is limited.	Student's accuracy with vocabulary and structures is adequate.	Student's accuracy with vocabulary and structures is exemplary.
Comprehensibility	Student's ideas lack clarity and are difficult to understand.	Student's ideas are adequately clear and fairly well understood.	Student's ideas are precise and easily understood.
Vocabulary Use	Student uses limited and repetitive vocabulary.	Student uses only recently acquired vocabulary.	Student uses both recently and previously acquired vocabulary.

Las rosas de Casilda

En el año 711, los moros del norte de África invadieron a España y durante ocho siglos *(centuries)* gobernaron en muchas partes del país hasta su expulsión por los reyes católicos, Isabel y Fernando, en 1492. Durante estos años, había peleas constantes entre los moros y los cristianos. Había moros y cristianos crueles, pero también había muchos que eran buenos.

1 En el siglo XI vivía en Toledo un rey moro que se portaba muy mal con los cristianos. En todo el país tenía fama de ser muy cruel. Pero su hija, la princesa Casilda, era buena, obediente y generosa. Ella se comportaba bien con la gente. Tenía todas las cualidades que a su padre le faltaban. También era una joven muy bonita.

2 El rey se llamaba Al-Mamún, y él y la princesa vivían en el alcázar de Toledo. (Un alcázar es el nombre árabe de un palacio.) Además de tener cientos de cuartos y salas, el alcázar tenía una prisión en el sótano para los prisioneros políticos y religiosos. Cuando salía victorioso, el rey Al-Mamún capturaba a los cristianos y los llevaba a la prisión en el horrible sótano del alcázar. Allí, las familias estaban separadas y todos —hombres, mujeres, niños y ancianos— fueron torturados. Sufrían mucho. Gritaban y lloraban constantemente, pero sobre todo por la noche, mientras los que vivían en el alcázar estaban durmiendo.

3 Una noche, los gritos despertaron a la princesa Casilda. La buena mora se levantó y decidió investigar lo que pasaba. Casilda llegó a la puerta de la prisión y vio a los pobres prisioneros. Vio que tenían hambre, y que algunos estaban mal heridos. Le dio mucho pena, pero no hizo nada.

4 Al día siguiente, le preguntó a su padre: —Querido padre, ¿por qué gritan y lloran los prisioneros? ¿Por qué no tienen ni comida para su hambre ni medicinas para curar sus heridas?

5 —¡No me preguntes esto! ¡Son mis prisioneros! ¡Y no vuelvas a bajar a la prisión! ¡Te lo prohíbo! —contestó el rey, furioso.

6 Pero la visión de los prisioneros —sobre todo la de los niños— le quitaba el sueño a Casilda. No podía dormir, pensando en ellos. Y aquella misma noche, mientras todos estaban durmiendo, Casilda bajó a la cocina del alcázar, buscó pan y otros alimentos y escondió todo dentro de su larga falda. Volvió a la prisión con la comida. Al día siguiente —y por la noche— bajó a la prisión con más comida y con algunas medicinas. Así pasaba Casilda los meses de la primavera y del verano.

7 Un día su padre el rey tuvo que irse de viaje. Iba a estar ausente unas semanas. Durante el viaje del rey, Casilda visitaba a los prisioneros de día. Pero una tarde mientras Casilda les llevaba comida y medicinas escondidas en su falda, llegó al alcázar su padre.

8 —¿Qué haces, Casilda? —preguntó el rey—. ¿Y qué llevas en la falda?

9 Casilda estaba paralizada de miedo. Ella sabía lo cruel que era su padre con todos los que no le obedecían. Con mucho miedo, entonces, la princesa contestó: —Padre, son sólo unas rosas del jardín.

10 —No me mientas, hija. ¡Quiero ver lo que tienes ahora mismo! —gritó el rey.

11 Casilda no podía esconder lo que llevaba. Temblando, ella abrió la falda pero no había ni comida ni medicina. En su lugar, ¡había unas preciosas rosas rojas!

12 Ocurrió un <u>milagro</u> y el rey lo sabía. Esta misma tarde, Al-Mamún puso en libertad a todos los prisioneros y terminó para siempre las peleas con los cristianos.

Practice Test

Answer questions 1–6. Base your answers on the reading *"Las rosas de Casilda."*

1 Casilda and her father lived in

A a dark basement of the palace.
B North Africa.
C Al-Mamún.
D an *alcázar.*

2 Which of the following statements is not true?

F The prisoners suffered a great deal.
G The prisoners were tortured.
H Families were separated in prison.
J Many prisoners were executed.

3 The king's behavior changed because

A of how the food and medicine changed into roses.
B his armies were victorious.
C the prisoners escaped from prison.
D he saw the food and medicine Casilda had hidden.

4 What does the word *milagro* mean in paragraph 12?

F conflict
G a kind of flower
H miracle
J military victory

5 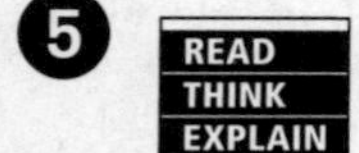

Describe how you think Casilda was affected by seeing the prisoners.

6 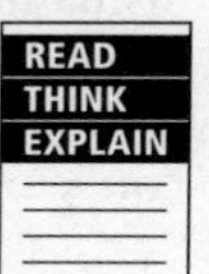

Casilda no obedeció a su padre porque ella siempre bajaba a la prisión para ayudar a los prisioneros. ¿Es importante siempre obedecer? Describe los momentos en los que hay que obedecer y en los que no es necesario seguir las reglas.

Realidades 2 Nombre Fecha

Tema 5

Practice Test Answer Sheet

1 Ⓐ Ⓑ Ⓒ Ⓓ 2 Ⓕ Ⓖ Ⓗ Ⓙ 3 Ⓐ Ⓑ Ⓒ Ⓓ

4 Ⓕ Ⓖ Ⓗ Ⓙ

5

READ, THINK, EXPLAIN

6

READ, THINK, EXPLAIN

Determining the Author's Point of View

To determine the author's point of view in a reading selection, the reader must figure out how the author feels about a subject in the reading selection. To begin with, readers should be able to identify when an author feels positive, negative, or neutral toward a subject. As you gain more practice with this skill, you should be able to identify a wide range of emotions or attitudes shown by authors. Some of these might include admiration, nostalgia, sarcasm, surprise, and sympathy.

Tip

To figure out the author's point of view toward his subject, try to locate words, phrases, or sentences in the text that have positive or negative associations or connotations. For example, consider the words listed below. Which one of the words sounds more positive? Which sounds more negative? Which sounds more neutral?

Column A	Column B	Column C
1. denim pants	**1.** faded jeans	**1.** hand-me-downs
2. cafeteria food	**2.** lunch time	**2.** five-star meal
3. classic car	**3.** used car	**3.** mid-size car

1. On page 299 in your textbook, review **Actividad 6,** ***La nueva reina.*** Look at the phrases below from the passage and place a **+** sign next to any phrase that has positive connotations, a **–** sign next to any phrase with negative connotations, and a **0** next to any phrase where the connotations seem to be neutral.

_________ *la gente se volvía loca*

_________ *nativa de Zacatecoluca*

_________ *una joven talentosa y bonita*

_________ *participó en la competencia de talento*

_________ *una voz fenomenal*

_________ *visitar a personas enfermas y heridas*

Sample question:

2. In the newspaper article titled *"Felicitaciones a la Señorita Centroamérica,"* which word best describes the author's point of view toward the newly crowned beauty queen?

A indifferent
B sarcastic
C admiring
D surprised

Reading Skills: Lectura, pp. 310–311

Making and Confirming Inferences

One mark of good readers is their ability to read between the lines of a text. Not only do they literally read and comprehend what a text says, but they also make inferences from what they read. An inference is an educated guess about something written in the text. An inference, because it is a guess, can never be absolutely right or wrong. However, an inference, like a conclusion, can be believable based upon the evidence that is present in the text. Confirming an inference means locating the evidence in the text that lends support to the inference.

Tip

One strategy that helps students as they make and confirm inferences is a two-column note activity known as Opinion-Proof. As you read, you formulate educated guesses or opinions about what you have read. You write these down on the Opinion side of your notes. If your opinions are believable, then you should be able to write down on the Proof side all the evidence you find in the reading passage that lends support to your opinion or inference.

1. On pages 310 and 311 in your textbook, read the **Lectura, *Los Juegos Panamericanos.*** Based on what you have read, fill in the missing blanks of the Opinion-Proof chart below.

Opinion	Proof
	El logotipo de los Juegos Panamericanos de Guadalajara 2011 es una llama de fuego que representa a las Américas y al deporte olímpico. Tiene cuatro colores: tres corresponden a los colores de los aros olímpicos y el magenta hace referencia a México.
The mascots Lobi and Cauê seem designed to make the participants at the Pan American Games feel welcome.	

Sample question:

2. Based on the information concerning the motto, logo, and mascots of the Pan American Games, one can infer that
   - **A** the strongest countries are recognized by winning the most gold medals.
   - **B** friendship and cooperation are at the heart of the Pan American Games.
   - **C** competing in sports has kept the countries of the Americas away from war.
   - **D** the name of Havana's *Tocopan* is a combination of the word *tocororo*, which is Cuba's national bird, and the word *Panamericanos*.

Realidades 2

Capítulo 6A

Integrated Performance Assessment

Unit theme: ¿Viste el partido en la televisión?

Context for the Integrated Performance Assessment: Your Spanish teacher would like to know more about his/her students' interests, especially the kinds of programs they like to watch on television. He has asked the students to give a presentation on what they do and do not like to watch.

Interpretive Task: Watch the *Videohistoria: El partido final* from *Realidades 2, DVD 3, Capítulo 6A.* Do you like interview programs? Do you like sports broadcasts?

Interpersonal Task: In a group of 2 or 3 students, brainstorm different kinds of TV programs. Give examples of each kind of program. Discuss the kinds of shows you like and do not like and explain why.

Presentational Task: Make an oral presentation to the class describing two kinds of TV programs you like. Give specific examples of each kind of program and explain why you like them. Include a description of a type of show you do not like and explain why.

Interpersonal Task Rubric

	Score: 1 Does not meet expectations	**Score: 3 Meets expectations**	**Score: 5 Exceeds expectations**
Language Use	Student uses little or no target language and relies heavily on native language word order.	Student uses the target language consistently, but may mix native and target language word order.	Student uses the target language exclusively and integrates target language word order into conversation.
Vocabulary Use	Student uses limited and repetitive language.	Student uses only recently acquired vocabulary.	Student uses both recently and previously acquired vocabulary.

Presentational Task Rubric

	Score: 1 Does not meet expectations	**Score: 3 Meets expectations**	**Score: 5 Exceeds expectations**
Amount of Communication	Student gives limited or no details or examples.	Student gives adequate details or examples.	Student gives consistent details or examples.
Accuracy	Student's accuracy with vocabulary and structures is limited.	Student's accuracy with vocabulary and structures is adequate.	Student's accuracy with vocabulary and structures is exemplary.
Comprehensibility	Student's ideas lack clarity and are difficult to understand.	Student's ideas are adequately clear and fairly well understood.	Student's ideas are precise and easily understood.
Vocabulary Use	Student uses limited and repetitive vocabulary.	Student uses only recently acquired vocabulary.	Student uses both recently and previously acquired vocabulary.

Reading Skills: Actividad 16, p. 330

Determining the Main Idea

To determine the main idea of a reading passage, you must be able to describe what a reading passage is mostly about and to summarize it in one sentence. A common problem for students when working with this skill is confusing an important detail in the reading passage with the main idea. Just because something is mentioned in the reading passage does not mean it is the main idea of the passage. In fact, many times the main idea is not even stated in the reading passage. This is often called an implied main idea. No matter if the main idea is stated or implied, the basic question remains the same: "What is this reading passage mostly about?"

Tip

One common mistake that students make with main idea questions is that they often choose main idea statements that are either too broad or too narrow. When you are too broad in your thinking, you do not recognize what is unique about the particular reading passage. When you are too narrow, you focus too much on isolated details without looking at the whole picture.

1. Review **Actividad 16, *Los premios ALMA*** on page 330 in your textbook. Then read the main idea statements listed below, and indicate if they are too broad, too narrow, or just right.

_______________ Awards programs recognize the top talents in many industries.

_______________ Some of the stars that have received ALMA awards include Jimmy Smits, America Ferrera, and Andy García.

_______________ The ALMA awards were established in 1995.

_______________ ALMA is an awards program that was established to help promote a fair and balanced representation of Latin people in film, television, and music.

_______________ In the film category, ALMA presents awards to Latin directors, actors, and actresses that produce films in English for the American audience.

_______________ The success of Latin professionals in many fields proves that it is hard to portray the Latin experience in the United States with stereotypical characters.

Sample question:

2. Another good title for the reading passage ***"Los premios ALMA"*** would be
   A "1995—The Birth of ALMA."
   B "Awards Programs in the United States."
   C "ALMA Rewards Those Who Portray Latin People Fairly."
   D "ALMA Recognizes Jimmy Smits, America Ferrera, Andy García, and Others."

Reading Skills: Lectura, pp. 336–337

Determining the Author's Point of View

To determine the author's point of view in a reading selection, the reader must figure out how the author feels about a subject in the reading selection. To begin with, you should be able to identify when an author feels positive, negative, or neutral toward a subject. As you gain more practice with this skill, you should then be able to identify a wide range of emotions or attitudes shown by authors. Some of these might include admiration, nostalgia, sarcasm, surprise, and sympathy.

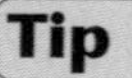

Tip

To figure out the author's point of view toward his or her subject, try to locate words, phrases, or sentences in which the author expresses an emotional reaction or an opinion. It helps to know how to distinguish facts from opinions.

1. Review the **Lectura,** ***La cartelera del cine*** on pages 336 and 337 in your textbook, paying special attention to the movie reviews under the headings of *"Sinopsis"* and *"Crítica."* Now examine the excerpts from the movie reviews listed below. Identify each as Fact or Opinion. Describe what the Opinions express about the author's feelings or attitude toward his or her subject.

Statement	Fact or Opinion	Feelings Expressed by Opinions
"Dinámica y entretenida, pero a veces incoherente, es importante ver esta película para conocer la historia de Magneto y el profesor X."		
"El programa Avatar le permite a Jake formar un cuerpo biológico controlado e infiltrarse entre los na'vi."		
"De la saga Batman, éste es el mejor trabajo hasta el momento."		
"Los efectos especiales nos llevan de viaje por un maravilloso mundo tropical de la ciencia ficción."		

Sample question:

2. The movie critic's point of view toward the film *"El caballero oscuro"* could best be described as
   A impressed with the action, the dialogue, and the acting in the movie.
   B disappointed with the film's special effects.
   C critical of the movie's plot.
   D enthusiastic about the film's themes of technology and the environment.

Realidades 2

Capítulo 6B

Integrated Performance Assessment
Unit theme: ¿Qué película has visto?

Context for the Integrated Performance Assessment: The entertainment editor of the Spanish language newspaper in your community is sponsoring an essay contest for students in local Spanish classes. The topic of the essay for students in Spanish 2 is "The Best Movie I Have Ever Seen." Since the newspaper will award passes to local movies for a year to the 20 students who write the best essays, you have decided to enter the contest.

Interpretive Task: Read the *Lectura: La cartelera del cine* on pages 336–337 of *Realidades 2.* Study the *sinopsis* and *crítica* for each movie. Decide what movie you will write about, and write a *sinopsis* and a *crítica* in draft form.

Interpersonal Task: Discuss your draft *sinopsis* and *crítica* with a friend in Spanish class. Give each other suggestions to improve your essays.

Presentational Task: Write the final draft of the *sinopsis* and the *crítica,* include a title, and submit your essay to the newspaper. Good luck!

Interpersonal Task Rubric

	Score: 1 Does not meet expectations	**Score: 3 Meets expectations**	**Score: 5 Exceeds expectations**
Language Use	Student uses little or no target language and relies heavily on native language word order.	Student uses the target language consistently, but may mix native and target language word order.	Student uses the target language exclusively and integrates target language word order into conversation.
Vocabulary Use	Student uses limited and repetitive language.	Student uses only recently acquired vocabulary.	Student uses both recently and previously acquired vocabulary.

Presentational Task Rubric

	Score: 1 Does not meet expectations	**Score: 3 Meets expectations**	**Score: 5 Exceeds expectations**
Amount of Communication	Student gives limited or no details or examples.	Student gives adequate details or examples.	Student gives consistent details or examples.
Accuracy	Student's accuracy with vocabulary and structures is limited.	Student's accuracy with vocabulary and structures is adequate.	Student's accuracy with vocabulary and structures is exemplary.
Comprehensibility	Student's ideas lack clarity and are difficult to understand.	Student's ideas are adequately clear and fairly well understood.	Student's ideas are precise and easily understood.
Vocabulary Use	Student uses limited and repetitive vocabulary.	Student uses only recently acquired vocabulary.	Student uses both recently and previously acquired vocabulary.

Ray Suarez

1 Entre los reporteros de televisión y radio más respetados de los Estados Unidos figura Ray Suarez. Suarez nació en 1957 y hace más de veinticinco años que es reportero. En ese tiempo ha trabajado en muchas de las principales ciudades del mundo.

2 Como reportero, Suarez es famoso por sus entrevistas de personas famosas y su análisis de eventos con impacto histórico. En su trabajo en programas de *talk radio,* Suarez también es excepcional por su talento especial para conversar con personas "comunes y corrientes" (*"ordinary"*) sobre cosas que son importantes para ellos. Su excelente trabajo le ha ganado muchos premios y honores. Entre los más importantes está el premio 1993/94 Alfred I. DuPont-Columbia University Silver Baton. Suarez ganó este premio por su programa de radio en NPR (*National Public Radio*), *Talk of the Nation,* que se transmitió desde Sudáfrica cuando, por primera vez, las elecciones en ese país incluyeron personas de todas las razas.

3 Otro honor ocurrió en octubre de 1999, cuando Suarez llegó a ser senior correspondent en el prestigioso programa, *The NewsHour with Jim Lehrer.* Este programa de noticias de televisión se transmite todas las noches de lunes a viernes por medio de PBS (*Public Broadcasting System*). Tiene un público de más de 3 millones de personas en todos los Estados Unidos.

4 Suarez nació Rafael Ángel Suarez, Jr. en Brooklyn, New York, de padres puertorriqueños. Estudió en New York University, donde su especialidad fue la historia africana. También estudió en la Universidad de Chicago, donde recibió su diploma de maestro en artes en estudios urbanos.

5 Suarez ha trabajado en Washington, D.C., Los Ángeles, Nueva York, Roma y Londres. También trabajó por siete años en Chicago, donde ayudó a fundar la organización Chicago Association of Hispanic Journalists. Fue voluntario con la YMCA de Chicago para ayudar a jóvenes pandilleros a abandonar su vida de crimen y violencia como miembros de pandillas, y empezar una vida nueva.

6 Además de su trabajo en *The NewsHour with Jim Lehrer,* Suarez escribe artículos y ensayos sobre temas políticos y sociales para varias revistas. En 1999, se publicó su libro, *The Old Neighborhood: What We Lost in the Great Suburban Migration, 1966–1999.* En este libro, Suarez examina por qué ya no existe un espíritu de comunidad en las grandes ciudades de los Estados Unidos. Habla francamente de problemas entre las razas en estas ciudades, y de cómo estos problemas contribuyeron a la migración de la gente blanca a los suburbios.

7 Una de las observaciones más interesantes de Suarez en *The Old Neighborhood* es sobre los latinos. Dice que los latinos en las grandes ciudades de los Estados Unidos son "invisibles" para los americanos, aunque están en todas partes haciendo los trabajos difíciles y necesarios para mejorar la vida de todos.

8 Algunas personas no estarán de acuerdo con esta observación, ni con otras de sus opiniones. Pero una cosa sí está clara: Ray Suarez va a seguir siendo muy visible, ayudando a su público a entender a las personas y los eventos —extraordinarios y no tan extraordinarios— de su tiempo.

Realidades 2

Tema 6 **Practice Test**

Answer questions 1–6. Base your answers on the reading *"Ray Suarez."*

1. According to the article, how does Suarez stand out in his work in the broadcast news field?

   A He can anticipate major political and social events.
   B He can talk easily with both famous and ordinary people.
   C He has an excellent memory and can make connections to other relevant topics.
   D He doesn't get flustered in tense situations.

2. What did Suarez do during South Africa's first all-race elections that won him a major award?

   F He eased tensions between the races.
   G He interviewed people on the street.
   H He made a documentary.
   J He broadcast his show from South Africa for that special event.

3. According to the article, what honor did Suarez receive as a television news reporter at the end of the last century?

   A a job as senior correspondent on *The NewsHour with Jim Lehrer*
   B the publication of his book, *The Old Neighborhood*
   C a prize for his help in establishing the Chicago Association of Hispanic Journalists
   D a second Alfred I. DuPont-Columbia University Silver Baton Award

4. In *The Old Neighborhood*, what does Suarez say about Hispanic Americans?

   F They should be welcomed and supported as new immigrants.
   G They should learn English as soon as possible.
   H Other Americans fail to realize the many contributions made by Hispanic Americans.
   J They should never forget their origins as they assimilate into the United States.

5. READ THINK CREATE ¿Qué pregunta te gustaría hacerle a Ray Suarez? ¿Por qué quieres saber esta información?

6. READ THINK EXPLAIN ¿Qué es lo que más admiras de Ray Suarez? ¿Por qué? Usa información y detalles del artículo en tu respuesta.

Tema 6

Practice Test Answer Sheet

1 Ⓐ Ⓑ Ⓒ Ⓓ 2 Ⓕ Ⓖ Ⓗ Ⓙ 3 Ⓐ Ⓑ Ⓒ Ⓓ

4 Ⓕ Ⓖ Ⓗ Ⓙ

5

READ
THINK
CREATE

6

READ
THINK
EXPLAIN

Reading Skills: Actividad 20, p. 362

Analyzing the Validity and Reliability of Information

When good readers analyze information for validity and reliability, one of the most important questions that they ask themselves is: "How do I know that I can trust that this information is true or accurate?" After answering this question, readers need to determine how such information can be used.

Tip

One way to check a reading passage for validity and reliability is to distinguish between the statements in the passage that are facts and those that are opinions. You generally trust factual information more than you trust opinions. A factual statement generally can be put to a test to prove whether the statement is true or false. Statements that involve numbers and/or measurements are more likely to be facts than opinions. Opinions are generally statements that could be interpreted differently by different people.

Let's look at two examples concerning food:

A Traditional Mexican food is delicious.
B Traditional Mexican food is likely to include corn and chiles.

It would be very difficult to prove the truth of Statement A because the word "delicious" is a value judgment. While many are likely to agree with Statement A, others, whose tastes are different, may disagree. Statement B, however, lends itself to a proof test. A survey of the food at traditional Mexican restaurants or interviews with experts in traditional Mexican cooking could provide the proof needed to recognize Statement B as a fact.

1. On page 362 in your textbook, review **Actividad 20 "*¡Se come bien aquí!*"** After you have finished reading, read the statements below and identify them as Fact or as Opinion.

_______________ ¡Se come bien aquí!
_______________ Se puede disfrutar de la major comida de la ciudad.
_______________ Tenemos los fresquísimos mariscos.
_______________ La comida mexicana moderna es el resultado de las influencias española y francesa con técnicas e ingredientes usados por los pueblos prehispánicos.
_______________ Se puede contemplar el arte más nuevo y bello de Jalisco.
_______________ Se abre diariamente a las 18:00 h.

Sample question:

2. Which statement from the advertisement for *Café de los Artistas* is likely to be most reliable?
   A You will eat well here.
   B You can enjoy the newest and most beautiful artwork of Jalisco here.
   C We have the freshest seafood.
   D We open daily at 6 o'clock in the evening.

Strategies to Understand Words and Text: Literal and Figurative Language

It is impossible to know the meaning of every word or expression in a language. However, good readers develop strategies to determine the meanings of unknown words or unusual expressions that they encounter in their reading without having to look all of them up in their dictionaries. Good readers also know that their guesses can often be wrong, so they develop strategies to check their guesses. When making an educated guess about an unusual word, good readers test their guess in context. In other words, they will insert their guessed meaning into the actual sentence where they encountered the unusual word.

Tip

Poems, even those written in the simplest forms, often confuse readers. Many poetic expressions can be interpreted in more than one way. On a first reading, a poem should be read on a literal level. For example, if a line in the poem says, "The sky was black," then you could imagine a sky filled with dark storm clouds.

However, on a second or third reading, you should consider the different ways those literal lines of poetry could be interpreted figuratively or creatively. For example, the line "The sky was black" might suggest that the sky was filled with migrating birds, or maybe it could suggest that the world seemed without hope on that day. Effective readers of poetry know that their figurative interpretations of individual lines must make sense in the overall context of the poem.

1. On pages 364 and 365 in your textbook, review the **Lectura** that contains the two poems by Pablo Neruda. Then complete the chart below for the selected lines of poetry.

	Literal Meaning	Possible Figurative Meanings
15 *el tomate, invade las cocinas,*		
25 *[el tomate] Tiene luz propia, majestad benigna.*		
28 *Debemos, por desgracia, asesinarlo;*		
41 *[el tomate] se casa alegremente con la clara cebolla,*		

Sample question:

2. In the poem *"Oda al tomate"* by Pablo Neruda, what is the most likely meaning of the line, *"En diciembre se desata el tomate, invade las cocinas..."*?
   - **A** Christmas, often represented by the color red, arrives every year in December.
   - **B** Every December, Chile's tomato festival is celebrated with a big outdoor tomato fight.
   - **C** Chile's first tomato crop arrives in December, and everyone buys the tomatoes.
   - **D** A flood of tomato-colored river water fills the streets of Chile in December.

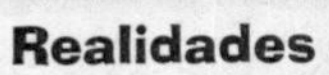

Realidades 2

Capítulo 7A

Integrated Performance Assessment

Unit theme: ¿Cómo se hace la paella?

Context for the Integrated Performance Assessment: The Spanish Club at your high school is getting ready to host a group of students from Spain who will arrive next month. The members of the club are planning a *fiesta de bienvenida* and you are on the food committee. You want to make the students feel at home, so you are thinking about making paella for the party.

Interpretive Task: Watch the *Videohistoria: ¿Cómo se hace la paella?* from *Realidades 2, DVD 4, Capítulo 7A.* Make a list of the ingredients that Ignacio and Javier buy and take notes on the preparation of paella. Afterwards, add the other ingredients for paella to your list.

Interpersonal Task: Work with the other members of the committee and compare your list of ingredients. Discuss the possibility of preparing paella for the party. Are the ingredients expensive? How much will you need to make? Is it difficult to prepare? Decide if you will prepare paella and explain your decision. If you decide on paella, discuss the other foods you will serve with it. If you decide not to serve paella, discuss and decide on other dishes.

Presentational Task: Make an oral presentation on the final decisions of the food committee to the members of the Spanish Club. Explain the reasons for your decisions.

Interpersonal Task Rubric

	Score: 1 Does not meet expectations	**Score: 3 Meets expectations**	**Score: 5 Exceeds expectations**
Language Use	Student uses little or no target language and relies heavily on native language word order.	Student uses the target language consistently, but may mix native and target language word order.	Student uses the target language exclusively and integrates target language word order into conversation.
Vocabulary Use	Student uses limited and repetitive language.	Student uses only recently acquired vocabulary.	Student uses both recently and previously acquired vocabulary.

Presentational Task Rubric

	Score: 1 Does not meet expectations	**Score: 3 Meets expectations**	**Score: 5 Exceeds expectations**
Amount of Communication	Student gives limited or no details or examples.	Student gives adequate details or examples.	Student gives consistent details or examples.
Accuracy	Student's accuracy with vocabulary and structures is limited.	Student's accuracy with vocabulary and structures is adequate.	Student's accuracy with vocabulary and structures is exemplary.
Comprehensibility	Student's ideas lack clarity and are difficult to understand.	Student's ideas are adequately clear and fairly well understood.	Student's ideas are precise and easily understood.
Vocabulary Use	Student uses limited and repetitive vocabulary.	Student uses only recently acquired vocabulary.	Student uses both recently and previously acquired vocabulary.

Reading Skills: Actividad 17, p. 385

Determining the Author's Purpose

To determine the author's purpose for writing a book, a story, an article, or any other text, the reader must figure out why the author wrote that particular book, story, article, or text. Some common purposes for writing are to inform, to entertain, to persuade, or to describe. Readers should also be able to explain why the author uses different techniques or includes different features within a text.

Tip

One common purpose for writing is to advertise a product, service, or organization. Advertising often includes a combination of different kinds of writing. An ad might begin with writing that grabs your attention. There might be descriptions of the product, service, or organization. There might be an explanation of what makes this product, service, or organization special. An ad might also include writing that tries to convince you to buy the product or service or to join the organization. Because ads are usually limited in size, every word included in an ad is there for a very specific reason.

1. On page 385 in your textbook, review **Actividad 17, *"El club de senderismo."*** For each of the sentences featured below, explain the author's purpose for including it in the advertisement.

	Author's Purpose
¿Te gusta dar una larga caminata por un sendero, hacer una buena fogata de leña, y dormir bajo las nubes...?	
El club de senderismo 'Aire puro' organiza excursiones al aire libre.	
No es necesario una preparación o condición física especial y hay muy poco peligro.	
***Aire puro** ¡Es la mejor manera de divertirse en la naturaleza!*	

Sample question:

2. Which sentence in the ad was most likely created to convince someone who might be fearful to join the hiking club *Aire puro*?
   A *El club de senderismo "Aire puro" organiza excursiones al aire libre.*
   B *Nuestro objetivo es combinar las actividades en la naturaleza con la cultura y el tiempo libre.*
   C *No es necesario una preparación o condición física especial y hay muy poco peligro.*
   D ***Aire puro,** ¡Es la major manera de divertirse en la naturaleza!*

Reading Skills: Lectura, pp. 390–391

Locates, Gathers, Analyzes, and Evaluates Written Information

By showing that they can locate, gather, analyze, and evaluate information from one or more reading passages, good readers demonstrate that they know how to conduct research. On a test, readers are often asked to locate, gather, analyze, and evaluate information from a reading passage, and then to show how to put that information to good use.

Tip

When conducting research, be sure to narrow your focus. As you read, you should often have a research question in mind. You should analyze what you are reading by asking, "Will the reading in this passage help me answer my research question?" If it will, highlight or underline the information or write the important details in your notes. By reading with a purpose, you are able to sort through all the different details in your reading and focus only on the information that relates to your research question.

1. Imagine that you were selected to lead a group of your fellow students on a hike through El Yunque National Park in Puerto Rico. You must prepare a speech about how they can be responsible hikers at the same time that they have an enjoyable time. Now, on pages 390 and 391 in your textbook, review the **Lectura, *El Yunque*.** For each detail in the reading included below, explain why you would or would not include that information in your speech.

	Why include or not include this in your speech?
El Yunque es una de las atracciones más visitadas de Puerto Rico.	
No toque las plantas del bosque.	
El coquí es una ranita que es un simbolo importante para los puertorriqueños.	
¡Venga y disfrute del parque!	
No abandone las veredas para no perderse.	

Sample question:

2. How would you respond to classmates who asked if your group could go swimming during your hike in El Yunque National Park?

A You would tell them that they could swim in the Mina Waterfall.
B You would tell them that swimming is not permitted in El Yunque National Park.
C You would tell them that swimming is only permitted in areas where the *coquí* does not live.
D You would tell them that they could swim only if they were camping in the park.

Realidades 2

Capítulo 7B

Integrated Performance Assessment

Unit theme: ¿Te gusta comer al aire libre?

Context for the Integrated Performance Assessment: You are going to Puerto Rico next month where you will live with a host family. Your host family is planning a variety of activities for you and one of them is a visit to *El Yunque*. They have sent you information on *El Yunque* and need some information from you. They want to know what you would like to see and do there and if you would like to camp there.

Interpretive Task: Read the *Lectura: El Yunque* on pages 390–391 of *Realidades 2*. Take notes on what you would like to see and do in *El Yunque*. Would you like to camp there? Why or why not?

Interpersonal Task: Tell your partner what you would like to see and do in *El Yunque*. Listen to what he/she would like to see and do. Talk about whether you want to camp there or not. Discuss your reasons. What questions do you have for your host family to help you prepare for your visit to *El Yunque*?

Presentational Task: Write an e-mail to your host family, telling them what you would like to see and do in *El Yunque*. Tell them whether you would like to camp there and explain why or why not. Ask them at least two questions.

Interpersonal Task Rubric

	Score: 1 Does not meet expectations	**Score: 3 Meets expectations**	**Score: 5 Exceeds expectations**
Language Use	Student uses little or no target language and relies heavily on native language word order.	Student uses the target language consistently, but may mix native and target language word order.	Student uses the target language exclusively and integrates target language word order into conversation.
Vocabulary Use	Student uses limited and repetitive language.	Student uses only recently acquired vocabulary.	Student uses both recently and previously acquired vocabulary.

Presentational Task Rubric

	Score: 1 Does not meet expectations	**Score: 3 Meets expectations**	**Score: 5 Exceeds expectations**
Amount of Communication	Student gives limited or no details or examples.	Student gives adequate details or examples.	Student gives consistent details or examples.
Accuracy	Student's accuracy with vocabulary and structures is limited.	Student's accuracy with vocabulary and structures is adequate.	Student's accuracy with vocabulary and structures is exemplary.
Comprehensibility	Student's ideas lack clarity and are difficult to understand.	Student's ideas are adequately clear and fairly well understood.	Student's ideas are precise and easily understood.
Vocabulary Use	Student uses limited and repetitive vocabulary.	Student uses only recently acquired vocabulary.	Student uses both recently and previously acquired vocabulary.

Flan de piña

El flan es un postre de natillas (custard) cocidas en su propia salsa de caramelo. Es muy popular en España y en México, y también se encuentra en los restaurantes de cocina hispana en los Estados Unidos.

Los ingredientes típicos del flan son azúcar, leche y huevos. Pero hay muchas recetas para hacer el flan, con diferentes ingredientes, medidas, tiempo de cocción y temperaturas, y recomendaciones sobre si es mejor prepararlo usando sólo el fuego de la estufa o el del horno también.

Esta receta contiene un ingrediente diferente muy sabroso y usa el fuego de la estufa y del horno. Como todo flan, éste se prepara en dos fases —primero el caramelo, y luego el flan.

Para hacer el caramelo

BATERÍA DE COCINA:

1 molde que se puede calentar en la estufa

INGREDIENTES:

$\frac{1}{2}$ taza de azúcar

1 cucharada de agua

PREPARACIÓN:

1. Se mezcla el agua con el azúcar en el molde y se calienta a fuego lento en la estufa. Cuando la mezcla esté brillante, se sube el fuego y se hierve la mezcla por unos minutos.
2. Cuando la mezcla tenga el color café claro del caramelo, se quita del fuego. Se inclina el molde por todos lados para que el caramelo quede por todo el fondo y los lados del molde. Se cubre el molde.

¡Ojo! ¡El azúcar se pone muy caliente y puede quemarle!

Para hacer el flan

BATERÍA DE COCINA:

1 cacerola que se puede calentar en el horno

1 olla

INGREDIENTES:

$1\frac{1}{2}$ tazas de jugo de piña (en lata)

$\frac{2}{3}$ de taza de azúcar

6 huevos

PREPARACIÓN:

1. Se hierven el jugo de piña y el azúcar en una olla, de 5 a 10 minutos, y después se enfría la mezcla.
2. Se baten los huevos y poco a poco se añaden a la mezcla en la olla.
3. Se pone la mezcla en el molde, y luego se pone el molde entero en una cacerola resistente al calor del horno. Se le pone agua caliente a la cacerola (¡no al molde!) hasta que el molde esté rodeado de agua, pero no sumergido. Se pone la cacerola con el molde al horno a 325°F por 50 o 60 minutos.
4. Se saca la cacerola del horno. Se saca el molde del agua, se enfría un poco y se pone en el refrigerador.
5. Cuando sea conveniente, se saca el molde del refrigerador, y se saca el flan del molde.
6. Se sirve el flan en seguida, o se devuelve al refrigerador hasta la hora de servirlo.

¡Buen provecho!

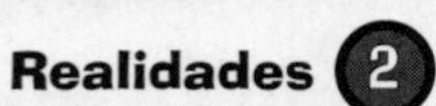

Practice Test

Answer questions 1–6. Base your answers on the reading *"Flan de piña."*

1 Which one of the following is not a typical ingredient in *flan*?

A milk
B eggs
C sugar
D pineapple

2 What is the meaning of *"batería de cocina"*?

F pots and pans
G baking goods
H battery-operated small kitchen appliances
J basic cooking utensils

3 According to the recipe, what do you have to watch out for as you are preparing the caramel?

A The caramel sauce might coat the bottom and sides of the mold.
B The sugar gets very hot and might burn you.
C The water might overflow from the pan holding the mold.
D The mix of sugar and water might get too bright and brittle.

4 Which kinds of heat are used for this recipe and when are they used?

F stovetop only for the entire recipe
G oven only for the entire recipe
H first oven, then stovetop
J first stovetop, then oven

5 READ THINK EXPLAIN

Nombra un ingrediente que te gustaría usar en una receta para flan. ¿En qué otros postres se usa ese ingrediente? ¿Es un ingrediente típico de postres americanos o de postres de otros países?

6 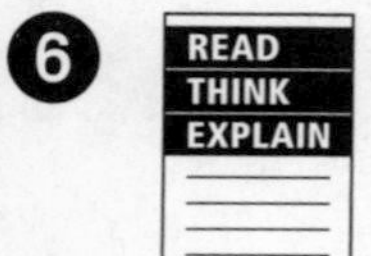

What do you think is the most important advice to give someone writing a recipe? What is the most important advice to give someone following a recipe? Explain your answers.

Realidades 2 Nombre ______ Fecha ______

Tema 7

Practice Test Answer Sheet

1 Ⓐ Ⓑ Ⓒ Ⓓ 2 Ⓕ Ⓖ Ⓗ Ⓙ 3 Ⓐ Ⓑ Ⓒ Ⓓ

4 Ⓕ Ⓖ Ⓗ Ⓙ

5

READ
THINK
EXPLAIN

6

READ
THINK
EXPLAIN

Reading Skills: Actividad 15, p. 412

Determining the Main Idea and Identifying Relevant Details

To know the relevant details in a reading passage is to know which ones are most important. The first step in identifying the relevant details is to identify the main idea of the passage. The relevant details are the ones that help support the main idea. After reading a passage, good readers ask themselves, "What is this passage mostly about?" and "Which details in the passage help support, explain, or prove the main idea?"

Tip

Good readers can often anticipate the important relevant details in a reading passage by formulating questions about the passage while they read. A good model for asking questions of the reading passage is to use the 5W (*Who, What, Where, When, Why*) 1H (*How*) questions of the journalist.

1. On page 412 in your textbook, review the article in **Actividad 15 *"¡Puedes sacarte un diez!"*** Answer the three questions that follow. Then formulate your own questions about the reading passage using the question words below. Make sure that you are able to answer the questions that you create.

Who might be impressed if you get a "ten" on your next test?

____

What feature must be present in the ideal study place?

____

Where are some bad places to study?

____

When ______________________________?

____

Why ______________________________?

____

How ______________________________?

____

Sample question:

2. Which is NOT a feature of developing good study habits?

A There should be a window in the ideal study place.
B A desk should be present in the ideal study place.
C Look out the window periodically to help you relax while studying.
D Avoid studying in the kitchen or in your bedroom.

Realidades 2 | Nombre ________ Fecha ________

Capítulo 8A | **Reading Skills: Lectura, pp. 418–419**

Determining the Main Idea

To determine the main idea of a reading passage, you must be able to describe what a reading passage is mostly about and to summarize it in one sentence. A common problem for students when working with this skill is confusing an important detail in the reading passage for the main idea. Just because something is mentioned in the reading passage does not mean it is the main idea of the passage. In fact, many times the main idea is not even stated in the reading passage. This is often called an implied main idea. No matter if the main idea is stated or implied, the basic question remains the same: "What is this reading passage mostly about?"

Tip

Sometimes readers are asked to identify the main idea, not of the entire reading passage, but of one small section of the passage. "Chunking" is one strategy that helps you better understand the main ideas of the different sections in a long reading passage. After dividing the reading passage into "chunks," or sections, you pause at the end of each chunk and try to summarize its main idea. After a chunk is summarized, you proceed to the next chunk and repeats the process until the entire passage has been read.

1. Review the **Lectura,** ***Ecuador: país de maravillas*** on pages 418 and 419 in your textbook. Then summarize each of the paragraph-long chunks listed in the chart below.

Paragraph beginning with ...	Main Idea
"Quito, la capital de Ecuador,…"	
"Declarada parte del patrimonio…"	
"A 30 minutos al norte de Quito…"	
"Dentro del monumento hay un museo…"	
"Ecuador le ofrece al visitante…"	
"Las islas Galápagos representan…"	
"La mejor manera de llegar a las islas…"	

Sample question:

2. The main idea of the fourth paragraph in the **Lectura,** ***Ecuador: país de maravillas*** could best be summarized as
   A a description of the museum located at the monument *La Mitad del Mundo.*
   B a description of some of the indigenous groups of Ecuador.
   C an explanation of why tourists should visit Ecuador's museums.
   D a story about the *salasacas* people.

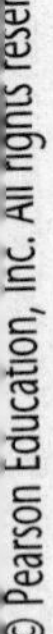

Realidades 2

Capítulo 8A

Integrated Performance Assessment

Unit theme: Un viaje en avión

Context for the Integrated Performance Assessment: You and a good friend have the opportunity to visit a Spanish-speaking country next summer. You both agree that you would like to go to Ecuador. Now you need to decide what you would like to see and do there.

Interpretive Task: Your Spanish teacher is thrilled that you are going to Ecuador! He/she has given you information about the country to help you make your plans. Read the *Lectura: Ecuador, país de maravillas* on pages 418–419 of *Realidades 2*. Take notes on what you would like to see and do in Ecuador and why.

Interpersonal Task: Discuss what you would like to see and do in Ecuador with your friend and listen to his/her ideas. Decide on at least 7 activities that you both would like to do. Discuss your reasons.

Presentational Task: Write a letter to your Spanish teacher telling what you have decided to see and do in Ecuador and explain why.

Interpersonal Task Rubric

	Score: 1 Does not meet expectations	Score: 3 Meets expectations	Score: 5 Exceeds expectations
Language Use	Student uses little or no target language and relies heavily on native language word order.	Student uses the target language consistently, but may mix native and target language word order.	Student uses the target language exclusively and integrates target language word order into conversation.
Vocabulary Use	Student uses limited and repetitive language.	Student uses only recently acquired vocabulary.	Student uses both recently and previously acquired vocabulary.

Presentational Task Rubric

	Score: 1 Does not meet expectations	Score: 3 Meets expectations	Score: 5 Exceeds expectations
Amount of Communication	Student gives limited or no details or examples.	Student gives adequate details or examples.	Student gives consistent details or examples.
Accuracy	Student's accuracy with vocabulary and structures is limited.	Student's accuracy with vocabulary and structures is adequate.	Student's accuracy with vocabulary and structures is exemplary.
Comprehensibility	Student's ideas lack clarity and are difficult to understand.	Student's ideas are adequately clear and fairly well understood.	Student's ideas are precise and easily understood.
Vocabulary Use	Student uses limited and repetitive vocabulary.	Student uses only recently acquired vocabulary.	Student uses both recently and previously acquired vocabulary.

Reading Skills: Actividad 7, p. 432

Locates, Gathers, Analyzes, and Evaluates Written Information

By showing that they can locate, gather, analyze, and evaluate information from one or more reading passages, good readers demonstrate that they know how to conduct research. On a test, readers are often asked to locate, gather, analyze, and evaluate information from a reading passage, and then to show how to put that information to good use.

Tip

Readers who conduct research are skilled at translating information from their reading into their own words. If you encounter information in one format, such as in a chart or in an essay, you should be able to restate that information in a different format such as in sentences or as bullets. This is how you demonstrate your comprehension of what you have read.

1. Review **Actividad 7** ***"Las vacaciones en Punta del Este"*** on page 432 in your textbook, and complete the chart using information from the reading passage.

Water Sport in Punta del Este	Rentals Available?	Other Important Information
Sailboating	Yes / No	
Jetskiing	Yes / No	
Windsurfing	Yes / No	
Waterskiing	Yes / No	

Sample question:

2. For which water sport can you find expert instructors to teach you at *el arroyo Maldonado* and at *la laguna del Diario*?
   - **A** sailboating
   - **B** jetskiing
   - **C** windsurfing
   - **D** waterskiing

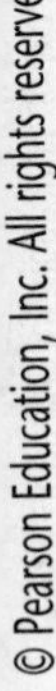

Reading Skills: Lectura, pp. 442–443

Identifying Methods of Development and Patterns of Organization

Good readers understand the tools and techniques of authors. To identify the methods of development used by an author in a text, you must first determine the author's purpose by asking, "Why was this text written?" After determining the author's purpose, you next ask, "What techniques did the author use to achieve his or her purpose?" These techniques are known as methods of development and could include, among other things, the organization pattern, the word choice, or the sentence structure used in the text.

Tip

One common purpose for writing is to create an advertisement. The travel brochure is a common type of ad, and good readers expect to encounter certain features in a travel brochure. Like all advertising, the travel brochure will likely begin with some attention-grabbing details concerning the advertised destination. Some of the writing will likely show what makes the advertised travel destination unique or special. The brochure will probably say something about the destination's history, its geographic location, its hotel and restaurant offerings, and its points of interest/tourist attractions.

1. On pages 442 and 443 of your textbook, review the **Lectura, *Antigua, una ciudad colonial***. Then answer the following questions.

How does the travel brochure grab the reader's attention?

____

What makes Antigua unique or special as a travel destination?

____

Which restaurant in Antigua is recommended? For what reasons?

____

What does the brochure say about Antigua's geographic location?

____

What are some details about Antigua's history?

____

What are some points of interest for tourists in Antigua?

____

Sample question:

2. Which sentence from the travel brochure best captures what is unique or special about Antigua as a travel destination?

A *Antigua le fascina al turista por sus calles de piedras, su arquitectura colonial y sus ruinas de iglesias y monasterios.*
B *¡Le invitamos a venir y a disfrutar de esta ciudad!*
C *La ciudad de Antigua tiene toda clase de restaurantes: desde restaurantes donde preparan platos guatemaltecos típicos hasta pizzerías.*
D *Desde el aeropuerto de la Ciudad de Guatemala, un avión lo lleva a Flores.*

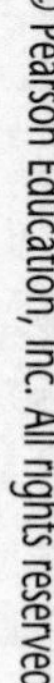

Realidades 2

Capítulo 8B

Integrated Performance Assessment

Unit theme: Quiero que disfrutes de tu viaje

Context for the Integrated Performance Assessment: A group of students from a Spanish-speaking country is coming to visit your school and community. They want to be sure that they behave appropriately during their visit. They have asked you for your advice.

Interpretive Task: Listen to Señora Milano as she gives her students advice on how to behave during their trip to Spain found on *Realidades 2, Audio Program DVD: Cap. 8B, Track 10*. (Don't worry about the directions given on the DVD itself. Use these directions instead.) As you hear her give advice to her students, think about what advice you will give the students coming to your community. Write down a few pieces of advice.

Interpersonal Task: Discuss advice to give the students coming to your community. Tell them what is important, good, and necessary that they do or not do and why. Give them advice on how to behave in both the school and the community. Work together until you have at least 8 pieces of advice.

Presentational Task: Write a note or e-mail to one of the students. Give him/her your advice on how to behave in your school and community. Explain the reason for each piece of advice.

Interpersonal Task Rubric

	Score: 1 Does not meet expectations	**Score: 3 Meets expectations**	**Score: 5 Exceeds expectations**
Language Use	Student uses little or no target language and relies heavily on native language word order.	Student uses the target language consistently, but may mix native and target language word order.	Student uses the target language exclusively and integrates target language word order into conversation.
Vocabulary Use	Student uses limited and repetitive language.	Student uses only recently acquired vocabulary.	Student uses both recently and previously acquired vocabulary.

Presentational Task Rubric

	Score: 1 Does not meet expectations	**Score: 3 Meets expectations**	**Score: 5 Exceeds expectations**
Amount of Communication	Student gives limited or no details or examples.	Student gives adequate details or examples.	Student gives consistent details or examples.
Accuracy	Student's accuracy with vocabulary and structures is limited.	Student's accuracy with vocabulary and structures is adequate.	Student's accuracy with vocabulary and structures is exemplary.
Comprehensibility	Student's ideas lack clarity and are difficult to understand.	Student's ideas are adequately clear and fairly well understood.	Student's ideas are precise and easily understood.
Vocabulary Use	Student uses limited and repetitive vocabulary.	Student uses only recently acquired vocabulary.	Student uses both recently and previously acquired vocabulary.

Practice Test

Dos atracciones turísticas de América Latina

El Parque Internacional La Amistad

1 Si visitas Costa Rica, puedes ver un sistema impresionante de parques nacionales, reservas indígenas y biológicas, y refugios para los animales salvajes. Gracias al Servicio de Parques Nacionales, que se estableció en 1970, más del 25 por ciento del país está reservado para la conservación. Por eso muchas especies que están en peligro de extinción en los países cerca de Costa Rica pueden vivir aquí.

2 Uno de los parques nacionales más interesantes es El Parque Internacional La Amistad, la reserva natural más grande de Costa Rica. Se llama internacional porque una parte del parque está situada en el país de Panamá. Hay mucha diversidad de hábitats y especies en el parque porque existe una gran variedad de altitudes y climas en esta zona. En el parque viven cinco tipos de <u>felinos</u>: el jaguar, el puma, el margay, el ocelote y el jaguarundi. También hay más de 200 especies de reptiles y anfibios y más de 500 especies de pájaros.

3 Turistas de todo el mundo van a Costa Rica todos los años para admirar esta maravilla tropical. Las visitas de estos turistas ayudan la economía del país y también contribuyen a la protección de sus recursos naturales.

Las islas Galápagos

4 Ecuador, situado en la parte oeste de América del Sur, es el país más pequeño de la región de los Andes. Gracias a su clima agradable y sus diversos hábitats, tiene una de las colecciones más extraordinarias de plantas y animales exóticos de todo el mundo.

5 Las islas Galápagos son parte de Ecuador; están en el océano Pacífico, a unas seiscientas millas de la costa ecuatoriana. Las islas Galápagos son un parque nacional y son famosas por los pingüinos, iguanas y tortugas gigantes que viven allí. Muchos de estos animales están en peligro de extinción. Para conservar el ecosistema del parque, hoy día se limita el número de personas que pueden visitarlo cada año. También se usa el dinero del turismo para proteger las diferentes especies que viven allí.

6 A los científicos les interesa mucho la flora y fauna de las islas Galápagos. En 1835, el naturalista inglés Charles Darwin llegó a las Islas como parte de una expedición científica de cinco años. Darwin se quedó en las Islas unos meses y estudió las plantas y animales que había allí y que no se encontraban en otras partes del mundo.

Practice Test

Answer questions 1–6. Base your answers on the reading *"Dos atracciones turísticas de América Latina."*

1 According to the reading, why is it possible for such a wide variety of species to exist in El Parque Internacional La Amistad?

- **A** The National Park Service imports exotic species from other countries.
- **B** It includes areas that have significant differences in altitude and climate.
- **C** Part of the park is in Costa Rica and part is in Panama.
- **D** Five zones of life are found in the park.

2 Why is it beneficial for the Galapagos Islands to be designated a national park?

- **F** It allows the park authorities to protect the ecosystem by limiting the number of visitors.
- **G** It allows the park authorities to charge more for admission.
- **H** It allows the park authorities to hire more park-certified guides.
- **J** It makes it more attractive as a tourist destination.

3 According to the article, which of the following is something that El Parque Internacional La Amistad and the Galapagos Islands do not have in common?

- **A** Both are national parks.
- **B** Both are popular tourist sites in their respective countries.
- **C** Both are associated with studies conducted by well-known scientists.
- **D** Both are home to diverse habitats and species.

4 In El Parque Internacional La Amistad, there are

- **F** more species of felines than reptiles.
- **G** more species of amphibians than birds.
- **H** more species of birds than reptiles.
- **J** about as many species of birds as there are reptiles.

5 READ THINK EXPLAIN ¿Por qué crees que algunos de los animales de las Islas Galápagos están en peligro de extinción?

6 READ THINK EXPLAIN Has visto que estas dos atracciones turísticas son muy populares. ¿Por qué es esto bueno y malo al mismo tiempo?

Realidades 2

Nombre ____________________ Fecha ____________

Tema 8

Practice Test Answer Sheet

1 Ⓐ Ⓑ Ⓒ Ⓓ 2 Ⓕ Ⓖ Ⓗ Ⓙ 3 Ⓐ Ⓑ Ⓒ Ⓓ

4 Ⓕ Ⓖ Ⓗ Ⓙ

5 READ THINK EXPLAIN

6 READ THINK EXPLAIN

Reading Skills: Actividad 22, p. 465

Recognizing Cause-Effect Relationships

To recognize cause-effect relationships in fiction, nonfiction, drama, or poetry, readers should be aware of why things happen (causes) as well as the consequences or results of actions (effects) in a reading passage.

Tip

Good readers can recognize when effects are presented in a reading passage. They also make predictions while they read and can predict the outcomes or effects of an action, even if the effects are not explicitly stated in a reading passage.

To gain practice with predicting outcomes, you should find places in the reading passage where you can stop and ask a "What if . . . ?" question. Such questions might lend themselves to more than one answer. Sometimes the answer to your "What if . . .?" question will be stated right in the reading passage. Other times, your question might be hypothetical and the acceptable answers will be the ones that make logical sense, even if they are not stated in the reading passage.

1. On page 465 in your textbook, review **Actividad 22 *"Los niños que trabajan."*** Then answer the "What if . . . ?" questions that follow. After answering each question, tell if the answer was in the reading passage or if you had to arrive at the answer logically.

   What if *El Programa del Muchacho Trabajador* had never been never started in Ecuador?

   ____

   ____

   What if child labor were not a problem in countries such as Ecuador?

   ____

   ____

   What if children did not work in the banana plantations of Ecuador?

   ____

   ____

   What if volunteers from around the world did not offer to help in *Los Espacios Alternativos*?

   ____

   ____

Sample question:

2. What would be the likely result if volunteers did not come to help *Los Espacios Alternativos*?
   A *Los Espacios Alternativos* would stop operating.
   B *Los Espacios Alternativos* would continue.
   C *El Programa del Muchacho Trabajador* would stop protecting the rights of child laborers.
   D The banana plantations would have to start hiring child laborers again.

Reading Skills: Lectura, pp. 468–469

Drawing Conclusions

To draw a conclusion is to form an opinion based on evidence. Sometimes the evidence presented to readers is very limited, but they must ensure that their evidence-based opinions make sense.

Conclusion statements are rarely right or wrong. They are often presented as believable or not. If you are successful at drawing conclusions from your reading, then you likely are skilled at finding evidence in your reading that supports your conclusions. Conclusions are only as strong as the evidence on which they are based. Conclusions based on little evidence are not as believable as conclusions based on a lot of different kinds of evidence. You must also be willing to change your conclusions as more evidence becomes available in the reading passage.

Tip

Readers must be flexible in their thinking when drawing conclusions from multiple and varied pieces of evidence. When the pieces of evidence are similar or the amount of evidence is limited, drawing conclusions is not difficult.

1. In the **Lectura,** ***¡Descubre tu futuro!*** on pages 468 and 469 of your textbook, review the test *"Una prueba de aptitud."* Below you will find excerpts from the test questions that will serve as pieces of evidence. For each set of evidence, draw a conclusion about the person's future career that makes sense.

   A *A Miguel le gusta trabajar con animales, máquinas y herramientas.*
   B *Miguel prefiere cosas prácticas que se pueden tocar y ver.*
   Conclusion about Miguel's future career: ______________________________
   ____

   A *Laura evita situaciones sociales.*
   B *Laura prefiere la política y los negocios.*
   Conclusion about Laura's future career: ______________________________
   ____

   A *Victor es emprendedora.*
   B *A Victor le gusta ser el líder.*
   C *Victor prefiere ayudar a otras personas.*
   Conclusion about Victor's future career: ______________________________
   ____

Sample question:

2. Which conclusion below is LEAST credible about a person who would choose letter A responses for all the questions on the test *"Una prueba de aptitud"*?
   A Such a person might prefer working as a party planner.
   B Such a person might enjoy working as a zoo keeper.
   C Such a person would enjoy a hands-on job more than an office job.
   D Such a person might not be interested in a job filled with idealism.

Integrated Performance Assessment

Unit theme: ¿Qué profesión tendrás?

Context for the Integrated Performance Assessment: You are on your school's yearbook committee. You have decided to have your classmates write about what they will do in the future.

Interpretive Task: Watch the *Videohistoria: Y tú, ¿qué vas a ser?* from *Realidades 2, DVD 4, Capítulo 9A.* As you listen, think about your future. What kind of career will you have? Why? Where will you live? Why? Will you get married?

Interpersonal Task: Discuss your plans for the future with a friend in Spanish class. What additional information can you add to your plans for the future?

Presentational Task: Write your description of your plans for the future for the yearbook.

Interpersonal Task Rubric

	Score: 1 Does not meet expectations	Score: 3 Meets expectations	Score: 5 Exceeds expectations
Language Use	Student uses little or no target language and relies heavily on native language word order.	Student uses the target language consistently, but may mix native and target language word order.	Student uses the target language exclusively and integrates target language word order into conversation.
Vocabulary Use	Student uses limited and repetitive language.	Student uses only recently acquired vocabulary.	Student uses both recently and previously acquired vocabulary.

Presentational Task Rubric

	Score: 1 Does not meet expectations	Score: 3 Meets expectations	Score: 5 Exceeds expectations
Amount of Communication	Student gives limited or no details or examples.	Student gives adequate details or examples.	Student gives consistent details or examples.
Accuracy	Student's accuracy with vocabulary and structures is limited.	Student's accuracy with vocabulary and structures is adequate.	Student's accuracy with vocabulary and structures is exemplary.
Comprehensibility	Student's ideas lack clarity and are difficult to understand.	Student's ideas are adequately clear and fairly well understood.	Student's ideas are precise and easily understood.
Vocabulary Use	Student uses limited and repetitive vocabulary.	Student uses only recently acquired vocabulary.	Student uses both recently and previously acquired vocabulary.

Reading Skills: Actividad 20, p. 489

Strategies to Analyze Words: Context Clues

It is impossible to know the meaning of every word in a language. Good readers develop strategies to determine the meanings of unknown words as they read without having to look them up in the dictionary. In using context clues, good readers examine the sentences surrounding new vocabulary words looking for clues that might help them guess the meaning of the new word.

Tip

With an understanding of sentence structure, context clues are easier to find and use. One common sentence pattern contains two clauses that have an opposite relationship. This can be illustrated using any of the following conjunctions (in boldface):

—**Although** Madrid is a beautiful city, its late-night noises can be disturbing to tourists.
—**While** Madrid is a beautiful city, its late-night noises can be disturbing to tourists.
—Madrid is a beautiful city, **but** its late-night noises can be disturbing to tourists.
—Madrid is a beautiful city; **however**, its late-night noises can be disturbing to tourists.

When you encounter an unusual word in one of the two clauses, the context of the sentence tells you that the unusual word will have an opposite relationship to words in the other clause.

1. In **Actividad 20** ***"La contaminación acústica,"*** on page 489 in your textbook, you will find the following sentence:

   Para unos el ruido de una motocicleta puede ser agradable, ***mientras que*** *para otros resulta un ruido que detestan.*

   If you did not know the meaning of the word *agradable*, but you did recognize the conjunction *mientras que* in this sentence, context clues would tell you that *agradable* must be opposite in nature to *un ruido que detestan*. What is the meaning of *agradable*?

Sample question:

2. Read the sentences below and then choose the best meaning for the underlined word.

   For those who love city life, the combined sounds of subways rumbling underground, police sirens piercing the night air, and jet engines roaring across the sky might seem a symphony. However, to one unaccustomed to such sounds, the noises of city life would likely be a <u>cacophony</u>.

   A a blending of harmonious sounds
   B an orchestral arrangement of classical music
   C harsh or discordant sounds
   D jet engines roaring across the sky

Reading Skills: Lectura, pp. 492–493

Locates, Gathers, Analyzes, and Evaluates Written Information

By showing that they can locate, gather, analyze, and evaluate information from one or more reading passages, good readers demonstrate that they know how to conduct research. On a test, readers are often asked to locate, gather, analyze, and evaluate information from a reading passage and then show how to put that information to good use.

Tip

Readers who conduct research often read with a purpose. That means that you have a research question or problem in your head while you read. If you encounter information in a reading passage that relates to your research question or problem, you should underline, selectively highlight, or write notes about that information. Later you should come back to those sections to analyze and evaluate the information to determine if it will be useful to your research.

1. On pages 492 and 493 in your textbook, re-read the **Lectura,** ***Protejamos la Antártida.*** After you finish reading, consider the following scenario: Imagine that you and some classmates are working on a community service project to increase understanding of global warming. Now look at the excerpts from the **Lectura** below and explain why this information would or would not be useful for your community service project.

	Useful or Not Useful? Why?
La Antártida es un desierto frígido donde casi nunca llueve.	
Las regiones polares son muy importantes para la supervivencia de la Tierra entera.	
Cuando se destruyen las casquetes de hielo en las zona polares, hay menos luz solar que se refleja y la Tierra se convierte en un receptor termal.	
A través de los años, muchos países han declarado soberanía de derechos sobre la Antártida y esto ha producido problemas, especialmente en Argentina y Chile.	

Sample question:

2. Which information from the reading passage would be most useful to someone writing a report about Antarctica and global warming?
   A The Antarctic Treaty established rules for the use of the region.
   B It was in Antarctica that holes in the ozone layer were first discovered in 1985.
   C Ninety percent of the ice on earth can be found in Antarctica.
   D The existence of species in Antarctica is limited by the climate and the ice, but there exists an abundance of life in the surrounding waters.

Realidades 2

Capítulo 9B

Integrated Performance Assessment

Unit theme: ¿Qué haremos para mejorar el mundo?

Context for the Integrated Performance Assessment: It's Environmental Awareness Month at your high school and the sponsor of your Spanish Club has received a brochure from an organization called *¡Protejamos la Antártida!* (Let's Protect Antarctica!). The brochure asks for donations to the organization and your sponsor wants to know if the members of the club would like to raise funds to send to the organization.

Interpretive Task: Read the *Lectura: Protejamos la Antártida* on pages 492–493 of *Realidades 2* and take notes on the importance of Antarctica . Do you think your Spanish Club should raise funds for *¡Protejamos la Antártida!?* Why or why not?

Interpersonal Task: Work with a group of students who share your opinion. Discuss your reasons for wanting or not wanting to raise funds for the organization. Do you need more information before you can make a decision? If so, what do you want to know? If you choose not to raise funds for *¡Protejamos la Antártida!*, what kind of environmental organization are you willing to support? Prepare to present and defend your point of view.

Presentational Task: Present your decision to the other members of the Spanish Club. Tell them if you want to raise funds for *¡Protejamos la Antártida!* or not. If so, why? If not, why not? What kind of environmental organization are you willing to support? Why? In either case, suggest how the club might raise the money.

Interpersonal Task Rubric

	Score: 1 Does not meet expectations	**Score: 3 Meets expectations**	**Score: 5 Exceeds expectations**
Language Use	Student uses little or no target language and relies heavily on native language word order.	Student uses the target language consistently, but may mix native and target language word order.	Student uses the target language exclusively and integrates target language word order into conversation.
Vocabulary Use	Student uses limited and repetitive language.	Student uses only recently acquired vocabulary.	Student uses both recently and previously acquired vocabulary.

Presentational Task Rubric

	Score: 1 Does not meet expectations	**Score: 3 Meets expectations**	**Score: 5 Exceeds expectations**
Amount of Communication	Student gives limited or no details or examples.	Student gives adequate details or examples.	Student gives consistent details or examples.
Accuracy	Student's accuracy with vocabulary and structures is limited.	Student's accuracy with vocabulary and structures is adequate.	Student's accuracy with vocabulary and structures is exemplary.
Comprehensibility	Student's ideas lack clarity and are difficult to understand.	Student's ideas are adequately clear and fairly well understood.	Student's ideas are precise and easily understood.
Vocabulary Use	Student uses limited and repetitive vocabulary.	Student uses only recently acquired vocabulary.	Student uses both recently and previously acquired vocabulary.

Español, el idioma del futuro

1 De los más de 3,500 idiomas que se hablan, el español es, según algunas estadísticas, el tercer idioma más hablado, y según otras, es el cuarto. El chino es el idioma que más personas hablan y luego está el hindi; el inglés y el español compiten por el tercer lugar. Hay alrededor de 400 millones de hispanohablantes en el mundo. El español es el idioma oficial de más de 20 países y se habla en todos los continentes: Europa, América, África, Asia (hay muchos filipinos que lo hablan), Oceanía (en la Isla de Pascua de Chile) y Antártida (donde Argentina y Chile tienen bases científicas). A estos 400 millones, hay que añadir casi 100 millones más que lo hablan como segundo idioma.

En los Estados Unidos, la población
2 hispana sigue aumentando de manera constante. Según los datos del censo, el 13 por ciento de la población es hispano; para el año 2050 se estima que será el grupo minoritario más grande del país. El idioma que hablan los más de 39 millones de hispanos en los Estados Unidos tiene ahora una nueva importancia: capturar al consumidor de habla hispana. Los hispanos en los Estados Unidos han creado un nuevo y dinámico mercado, donde ya hay 48 canales de televisión en español, 460 emisoras de radio y 36 periódicos.

Es evidente que el español no solamente es
3 importante en los Estados Unidos. Por razones prácticas y económicas, es una de las <u>lenguas</u> que más se estudia como idioma extranjero fuera de España y de los países hispanos de América. En los Estados Unidos, por ejemplo, se estima que más de tres millones de jóvenes lo estudian. En el futuro, será importante saber los dos idiomas (inglés y español) para obtener un trabajo en muchas profesiones.

En Brasil hay cursos de español en
4 prácticamente todas las universidades del país. Casi 50 millones de brasileños (el 31 por ciento de la población) estudian español en las escuelas; es obligatorio estudiarlo en las escuelas secundarias. Y después del inglés, es la segunda lengua más hablada entre ejecutivos e industriales brasileños.

En los países europeos, más de 1,700,000
5 jóvenes estudian español en los diversos sistemas educativos. En Francia, es la segunda opción linguística en los colegios; la primera opción es el inglés.

En Japón hay 60,000 estudiantes
6 universitarios de español. Se ofrecen carreras en lengua española en 18 universidades y hay más de 115 centros de enseñanza de español. En Corea del Sur, lo estudian más de 20,000 estudiantes y hasta se ofrecen cursos de español en la radio.

En Australia, el español es el idioma europeo que más se estudia. Como hay,
7 además, 95,000 familias que hablan español en casa, no es sorprendente que haya en ese país tres periódicos en español.

Por eso, es vital que los que hablan español sepan su importancia, e intenten
8 conservar las tradiciones y la cultura de este grupo de hablantes que tiene un lugar tan importante en el mundo.

Practice Test

Answer questions 1–6. Base your answers on the reading *"Español, el idioma del futuro."*

1 The main idea of this article is to

- **A** give a brief history of the Spanish language.
- **B** explain where the reader can study Spanish.
- **C** describe the growing importance of the Spanish language.
- **D** give an overview of the most popular world languages.

2 Which of the following words is a synonym for *lenguas* in paragraph 3?

- **F** *profesiones*
- **G** *idiomas*
- **H** *gerentes*
- **J** *carreras*

3 According to the article, why do so many students study Spanish in Brazil?

- **A** It's similar to Portuguese.
- **B** It's one of Brazil's official languages.
- **C** Spanish classes are free.
- **D** Spanish classes are compulsory in high school.

4 Which of the following statements is not true?

- **F** Spanish can be heard on every continent.
- **G** Hispanics make up a relatively untapped market in the United States.
- **H** Hispanics are a growing minority in the United States.
- **J** South Korea offers Spanish lessons on the radio.

5 READ THINK EXPLAIN ¿Por qué crees que será importante saber inglés y español para obtener un trabajo en los Estados Unidos?

6 READ THINK EXPLAIN ¿Por qué tantas personas hablan español como segundo idioma? Usa información del artículo para justificar tu respuesta.

Nombre ______________________ Fecha ______________

Practice Test Answer Sheet

1 Ⓐ Ⓑ Ⓒ Ⓓ 2 Ⓕ Ⓖ Ⓗ Ⓙ 3 Ⓐ Ⓑ Ⓒ Ⓓ

4 Ⓕ Ⓖ Ⓗ Ⓙ

5

READ
THINK
EXPLAIN

6

READ
THINK
EXPLAIN

Notes

Notes

Notes